All the Dupes Fit to Print: Journalists Who Have Served as Tools of Communist Propaganda

Paul Kengor, Ph.D.

© 2013 by America's Survival, Inc.
All rights reserved. No part of this document
may be reproduced or transmitted in any form
or by any means, electronic, mechanical,
photocopying, recording, or otherwise,
without prior written permission
of America's Survival, Inc.

Published by
America's Survival, Inc.
P.O. Box 146
Owings, MD 20736
www.usasurvival.org 443-964-8208
Cliff Kincaid, President

Introduction by Cliff Kincaid, President, America's Survival, Inc.

Groups exist to monitor and reform higher education in general, and to critique the media, but with this report, America's Survival, Inc. (ASI) begins the process of reforming journalism education. This is consistent with our educational mission to expose threats to the American way of life and monitor extremist movements. A truly free press in America hangs in the balance.

We are particularly troubled by the influence of the group called "Free Press" in affecting the course of journalism education and encouraging the development of new media funded by the U.S. and foreign governments.

Robert McChesney is the socialist professor whose Free Press organization is leading the charge for the $50 billion "progressive" transformation of the media. Their aim is to keep liberal journalists employed at liberal media outlets and to put them to work in new "public media." The Free Press, funded by billionaire hedge fund operator George Soros, is urging "an alternative media infrastructure, one that is insulated from the commercial pressures that brought us to our current crisis."

Such a view rationalizes the acceptance of even foreign government-funded media such as Russia Today (RT) and Al Jazeera. The Free Press seems to welcome government funding or sponsorship of media organizations, even if the money comes from the Obama Administration, Qatar (sponsor of Al Jazeera) or Russia.

Indeed, at the 2013 Free Press conference, when I

tried to question McChesney about foreign propaganda channels entering the U.S. media market, he became visibly upset, grabbed my camera, and walked away in disgust, saying other people wanted to talk to him. All of this was captured on film. During the course of the conversation, such as it was, he tried to deny Al Jazeera's relationship with al Qaeda and other Muslim terrorist groups.

The Russian regime, which has a habit of murdering journalists and political opponents, has a covert and overt program of manipulation of the Western media, similar to what the old Soviet KGB used to specialize in. Demonstrating sensitivity to the charge that he is a paid Russian agent working in the progressive movement, radio host Thom Hartmann refused to discuss how much the Russians pay him to air his TV program "The Big Picture" on English-language Russia Today (RT). When I questioned him about this, he actually grabbed my camera recording his response in order to avoid being seen stonewalling.

Former KGB officer Konstantin Preobrazhensky has described the channel as a conduit for disinformation and propaganda from the Russian intelligence services.

Needless to say, it is fascinating and newsworthy that the modern-day progressive point of view is being openly broadcast by Moscow in the United States.

The mission of the Free Press is openly Marxist. In an article in the socialist *Monthly Review*, "Journalism, Democracy, and Class Struggle," McChesney declared, "Our job is to make media reform part of our broader struggle for democracy, social justice, and, dare we say it, socialism." John Nichols, a writer for *The Nation* and co-founder of Free Press, spoke at the November 2011 convention of the Democratic Socialists of America (DSA), a group that helped give Barack Obama his start in politics.

However, Free Press doesn't say one word about the well-documented liberal bias that has contributed to the decline in readers and viewers for traditional media outlets and has enabled the rise of the Fox News Channel, conservative talk radio, and the Internet.

As part of the proposed new "media infrastructure," Free Press is calling for a $50 billion "Public Media Trust Fund" to underwrite the creation of new jobs for journalists and the use of the existing federal AmeriCorps program "to include journalistic activities as part of its mission" in the form of "journalism positions" and "journalism projects." AmeriCorps is a federally funded national and community service agency.

The group is also urging a direct federal bailout of liberal media institutions, declaring that "The Department of Labor could design a program aimed at keeping reporters employed at existing news organizations or at new outlets." Free Press explains, "If the government were to subsidize 5,000 reporters at $50,000 per year, the cost would be $250 million annually, a relatively modest sum given the billions coming out of Washington."

In addition to the $50 billion "Public Media Trust Fund," another one of the proposals from the Free Press group is a $50 million "government-seeded innovation fund for journalism," described by Craig Aaron of Free Press as "a taxpayer-supported venture capital firm that invests in new journalism models."

The socialist nature of the proposals should not be surprising. Aaron is one of two Free Press staffers who have been employed by the socialist magazine *In These Times* and previously worked at Ralph Nader's Congress Watch. Aaron assumed a prominent role at a "Restore the Fourth" rally in Washington, D.C. on July 4, 2013, designed to support NSA leaker Edward Snowden, who fled to China and then Russia to escape espionage charges.

All of the controversial Free Press recommendations, which are finding a sympathetic ear in the Obama Administration, are included in the 185-page book, *Changing Media: Public Interest Policies for the Digital Age*.

The proposal represents a dramatic expansion of the more than 900 local public radio stations and more than 350 local public television stations which receive support from the taxpayer-financed Corporation for Public Broadcasting (CPB). The CPB, which supports the Public Broadcasting Service (PBS), PBS stations, and National Public Radio, receives approximately $450 million annually from federal taxpayers.

Public broadcasting entities have received over $8 billion from the taxpayers since their creation.

ASI is leading the effort to analyze what is being taught to journalism students around the country and to determine what can be done to bring balance to the curricula of journalism schools and journalism/communications departments. Burlington College in Vermont has gone further than just teaching left-wing journalism. Its booth at the 2013 "media reform" conference sponsored by Free Press advertised a degree in "media activism." The college says, "The degree is conceived explicitly for those who want to become media activists. Through technical training rooted in history and theory, students are encouraged to apply media making technique, craft, and art to issues of advocacy, activism and social change." This will be the wave of the future, if Free Press has its way.

As a graduate of the University of Toledo with a B.A. and major in communications and journalism, I understand the problem from personal experience.

My journalism textbook, *Interpretative Reporting*, which glorified liberal advocacy reporting, was written by Marxist journalism educator Curtis MacDougall. I obtained MacDougall's 300-page FBI file showing his long association with a series of Communist Party front groups. MacDougall was labeled one of the "makers of the media mind" in a book by William David Sloan. *Interpretative Reporting* was a standard text in journalism schools for more than 50 years, "used at one time or another by almost every journalism program in the country," Sloan noted.

MacDougall was investigated by the FBI because of his role as a fellow traveler of the Communist Party with ties to Soviet agents. He succeeded in poisoning the minds of many journalists.

His influence was felt not only on generations of journalists, but on his own son, A. Kent MacDougall, who came out openly as a Marxist after working at the *Wall Street Journal*. He said that he had inserted positive stories about Marxist economists and "the leftwing journalist I.F. Stone," later exposed as a Soviet agent. A. Kent MacDougall called Karl Marx his favorite journalist and said, "Reconciling radicalism and reporting for the mass media came naturally to me. I simply followed my father's lead."

Guardian columnist Glenn Greenwald, the mouthpiece and handler for NSA leaker Edward Snowden, accepted an "Izzy" award, named after I.F. Stone, from the Ithaca College Park Center for Independent Media. I had asked Glenn Greenwald, then with *Salon.com*, what he would say of an article in *Commentary* magazine about evidence linking Stone to Soviet intelligence. Rather than disavow the award, after he was informed about Stone's service to the Soviet Union, Greenwald attacked those, including myself, who had published evidence of Stone's work on behalf of the communist dictatorship.

We revealed evidence that Greenwald had addressed several Marxist-Leninist conferences over the last few years.

In fact, the conferences are officially sponsored by the Center for Economic Research and Social Change (publisher of International Socialist Review and Haymarket Books), and co-sponsored by The International Socialist Organization (publisher of Socialist Worker). The International Socialist Organization (ISO) is one of America's main Trotskyist/ Marxist-Leninist parties. It says, "We stand in the Marxist tradition, founded by Karl Marx and Frederick Engels, and continued by V.I. Lenin, Rosa Luxemburg and Leon Trotsky."

It was not clear if Greenwald is an actual member of the group or simply gives them aid and comfort. But a video of Greenwald's 2011 remarks, posted by the International Socialist Organization, shows him speaking in front of a big conference banner proclaiming socialism. In the talk, he defended WikiLeaks and Julian Assange against charges they illegally released classified information from Bradley Manning, the Army analyst who went on trial for espionage and aiding the enemy.

ASI will continue to document and expose cases of foreign manipulation of our media, including the activities of foreign propaganda channels Al-Jazeera and Russia Today.

In a sensational individual case, we disclosed that the late "CBS Evening News" anchorman Walter Cronkite is named in an FBI document from 1986 as being targeted in a Soviet "active measures" campaign against President Reagan's anti-communist foreign policy. Cronkite is named as a possible member of a U.S. delegation that would sign a pro-Soviet "People's Peace Treaty."

Cronkite, once known as "the most trusted man in television news" because of his influence during the time when three network news programs dominated the national dissemination of news and information, bears a great deal of responsibility for the American military defeat in Vietnam and the communist conquest of that Southeast Asian country.

The term "active measures" in the FBI document carries special significance because it designates Soviet intelligence operations to damage the United States and further the interest of Soviet foreign policy. The most common were political influence operations in which high-profile U.S. and Western political and public figures were used to promote Soviet objectives.

Released through the Freedom of Information Act (FOIA), the Cronkite documents include an FBI cover letter, dated June 25, 1986, which designates an attached internal memorandum from the "Campaign for a People's Peace Treaty" as part of a "Soviet active measures" campaign. The document is addressed to the FBI director and the attention of the Bureau's intelligence division.

In 1988, seven years after his retirement as anchorman of the "CBS Evening News", Cronkite had addressed a left-wing People for the American Way conference and denounced President Reagan for the "unilateral" military actions in Grenada, when the U.S. military evicted a communist gang, and Libya, when Reagan ordered a military strike in retaliation for the acts of terrorism against Americans. Cronkite despised Reagan's peace-through-strength policies and said that the smartest president he ever met was Jimmy Carter.

Later, Cronkite denounced Operation Iraqi Freedom and attacked the Bush administration for its "arrogance."

We found out after his retirement that he was not only a liberal, which was evident from his broadcasts, but a one-worlder. In appearances before the World Federalist Association, which favors world government financed by global taxes, he called for the U.S. to renounce "some of its sovereignty," pass a series of United Nations treaties, and create an "international Liberty Bell."

One of Cronkite's appearances, where he accepted a "Global Governance" award, is available on video on the America's Survival, Inc. YouTube channel, was at an event which featured the wife of then-U.N. boss Kofi Annan and a video from then-First Lady Hillary Clinton. The same "Global Governance" award had also been given to former *Time* magazine columnist Strobe Talbott, another advocate of world government who later became a top State Department official in the Clinton Administration and was subsequently named as a "special contact" of the Russian intelligence service by Russian master spy Sergei Tretyakov. Tretyakov is described as the highest ranking Russian intelligence official ever to defect while stationed in the U.S. and handled all Russian intelligence operations against the U.S. He served under cover from 1995-2000 at Russia's Permanent Mission to the United Nations but was secretly working for the FBI for at least three years. Talbott is now president of the liberal Brookings Institution.

Cronkite's role in the Vietnam defeat was reported after his death as if it were a highlight of his career. Yet, his misreporting helped create the conditions for a premature U.S. military withdrawal, leading to the loss of the lives of 58,000 Americans in vain, not to mention the millions of additional deaths caused in Vietnam and Cambodia by the Communists. Cronkite's public verdict that the 1968 Tet offensive was a "defeat" for the U.S. is widely seen as a turning point in American support for the war. Cronkite falsely claimed that the Vietcong had held the American embassy for six hours and that the offensive "went on for two months." The facts show that Tet was actually a major defeat for the communist enemy.

Beyond Vietnam, Cronkite got it wrong on the big issue of freedom versus Soviet communism. In the 1974 book, *TV and National Defense*, Dr. Ernest Lefever examined how CBS News programs for two years had covered national security issues and concluded that the news organization was "an active advocate of several national defense positions which were frequently critical of U.S. policy, and usually from a perspective that implied or called for a lesser military commitment and lower defense expenditures."

In 1972, for instance, the "CBS Evening News" aired nearly 1,400 presentations supporting the dovish view. Contrary or hawkish positions were aired only 79 times.

Asked about the charges, Cronkite displayed the bias that guided his news program, saying that "There are always groups in Washington expressing views of alarm over the state of our defenses. We don't carry those stories. The story is that there are those who want to cut defense spending." The "most trusted man in America" didn't deserve our trust.

In 1979, he gave an interview to the Soviet magazine, *Literary Gazette*, and told Vitaly Kobysh that the "Soviet threat" was "most likely . . . a myth." According to the magazine, Cronkite went on to say that "I will never believe in a 'Soviet threat.'"

Shortly after the interview was published, the Soviets invaded Afghanistan. He retired as "CBS Evening News" anchorman in 1981.

Cronkite told Accuracy in Media founder and editor Reed Irvine that he had been misquoted by Kobysh, and that he had a tape recording of the interview to prove it. The tape never materialized. Irvine ran into Kobysh at an international media conference and the Soviet journalist said the interview was entirely accurate.

After Ronald Reagan took office as President and proceeded to build up U.S. national defense capability, in the wake of the disastrous Jimmy Carter years, CBS News acted to counter the Reagan effort. They aired a five-part program, "The Defense of the United States," in which Cronkite appeared to tell us that the relationship with the Soviet Union was dominated by "the same old fears and doubts" because we didn't have a genuine dialogue with the Soviet communists.

Irvine noted at the time of the broadcast that CBS gave us "the Kremlin view that it is the United States, not the Soviet Union, that is striving for an impossible military superiority, while creating fantasies about Soviet aggression."

However, Irvine noted that Reagan "was not deterred" by the CBS News assault, but that the momentum behind his election mandate to rebuild America's defense was "weakened" somewhat by the constant repetition by the media that he was spending too much on national security. Cronkite's accomplices in this crusade included Dan Rather, his successor, and Bill Moyers, then with CBS and now with public television.

For many years Irvine drew attention to the "persistent anti-defense bias of CBS News" and reported, "One has to wonder why the anti-defense bias is so strong and persistent at CBS. My own feeling is that it is a reflection of the views enunciated by Walter Cronkite that show a benign view of the Soviet Union."

In 1989, Irvine expressed the hope that the Soviet archives would one day be opened to demonstrate how the Kremlin manipulated American journalists such as Walter Duranty of the *New York Times*, who had lied and helped Stalin cover up his monstrous crimes that resulted in the deaths of 7-10 million Ukrainians. Irvine added that "It will be fascinating to see what they say about Walter Cronkite, who spent two years in Moscow after World War II as a UPI correspondent and who has been remarkably restrained in his criticism of that country ever since."

This may sound harsh, but in addition to his role in America's Vietnam defeat, the fact is that Cronkite was consistently wrong about Soviet intentions, and his attitude dominated CBS News coverage of the old Soviet Union. Yet Cronkite has a journalism school named after him at Arizona State University.

This book by Paul Kengor begins the process of correcting the record about Cronkite and many other dupes in the journalism business.

We wish to thank Richard M. Scaife and his foundations for making this book and our journalism project possible.

Cliff Kincaid, President, America's Survival, Inc.

Chapter 1
"All the news that's fit to print."

That, of course, is the longtime motto of the *New York Times*, even as its pages for decades have featured the often questionable work of the likes of Walter Duranty and Herb Matthews, two reporters whose woefully misleading puff pieces on the likes of Joseph Stalin and Fidel Castro served as fodder for the Communist Party line, a line that ran from Moscow to Havana to, strikingly enough, Manhattan, where the headquarters of the *Times* sat not far from the headquarters of Communist Party USA (CPUSA) and the *Daily Worker*. While the *Times* has long been liberal/"progressive," and certainly not communist, readers could be forgiven for occasionally noticing lines in the *Times* not wildly different from the party line at *New Masses* or even *Pravda*. And when the *Times* did seem to toe the party line, it was not usually intentional; rather, it was usually a byproduct of well-intended liberal/progressive reporters being successfully misled by not-so-well-intended communist handlers.[1]

That, in fact, is what being duped is all about. Unfortunately, it is also about (at times) inadvertently doing the work of our adversaries. In being misled and manipulated, duped liberals/progressives in the American media have at times unwittingly served as tools of communist propaganda, and have thereby helped change the course of history in favor of America's adversaries.

Examples of this from the pages of the *Times* alone

are legion. I could fill this report strictly with examples from the Gray Lady. Take this colorful example from Oleg Kalugin, which would be hilarious if not so sad:

In the spring of 1959, Kalugin, a young Soviet citizen, found himself not in Moscow but New York City. He was completing a year's worth of study at Columbia University's School of Journalism. Somehow, the *New York Times* connected with the young man, or was connected to him (exactly how isn't clear). The *Times* was enamored with the young Russian, cobbling together a cheeky profile headlined, "A Popular Russian," which described this wide-eyed, wondrous man-on-the-street as "a real personality kid." Not only was the *Times* smitten, but so were the students and professors at Columbia, who described the beaming young man (so captured in the accompanying photo) as "brilliant." His wit and "engaging smile" had won him "many friends" at Columbia.[2] (*See* Appendix, Figure 1.)

For that matter, few colleges have been as far-left as Columbia University. The communist presence at Columbia was extremely strong. Young men as diverse as Whittaker Chambers and Thomas Merton entered the university as innocents and emerged as communists.[3] Professors like John Dewey and Corliss Lamont and others – some of them dupes, others outright communists or communist sympathizers – aided and abetted the indoctrination. When Mark Rudd and his SDS cohorts shut down Columbia in the 1960s – with Rudd en route to the Weather Underground as a fugitive fleeing the FBI for domestic terrorism – it seemed a fitting culmination of decades of Columbia radicalism. Thus, in 1959, it was hardly a surprise that the Columbia faithful would have swooned in the presence of Kalugin, a dynamic young Soviet.

Kalugin felt right at home at Columbia. "Part of the reason for his popularity at the School of Journalism," reported the *Times*, "has been his willingness to enter into the spirit of the work there." Kalugin "enjoyed" the school, and had "many tastes in common with his fellow students." He was already a member of the Young Communist League, explained the *Times* naively, and "expects to join the Communist party." The *Times* referred to the 24-year-old Kalugin as the innocent son of a Leningrad city clerk chosen for the Fulbright study exchange program by his sincere professors and "Soviet educational authorities."

Undoubtedly, few readers of this *Times* "Man in the News" article fully appreciated it quite like its subject. "I had to chuckle," admitted Kalugin many years later, after defecting to the United States. "It was all a lie. The Soviet educational authorities had not sent me to America.... The KGB had."[4]

Kalugin was not, as the venerable *Times* insisted to its faithful liberal/progressive readers (who surely sponged up the material), a bright young Soviet journalist. He was a bright young KGB officer, even as the *Times* reporter was an ignorant American journalist.[5] Kalugin was not the son of a hardworking city official but the son a man who worked for the Soviet secret police. And at the precise time of this *Times'* human-interest story, Kalugin was embarking on his first of many crucial espionage cases, all of which would quickly push him to the upper echelon of Soviet intelligence.

The *Times* concluded that Kalugin "thinks Soviet journalists can learn some things" from American journalists.

Chapter 2
Potemkin Progressives – by the boatload

Here was yet another case of *Times* reportage on communism managing to be a little off-base.

That said, it would be unfair to pick (solely) on the *New York Times*. The *Times* is hardly unique to such duping, even as its readers afford the *Times* an almost sacred status: *Give us this day our New York Times.* So, in a sense, to highlight the *New York Times*, or focus on it exclusively, would not be wholly inappropriate.

This report, however, looks at a variety of examples of newspapers and journalists from many different sources and from way back. Indeed, one can go to the very launch of the Bolshevik Revolution in 1917 and the American Communist Party in 1919. In no time, America's progressives were happily hailing the "Great Experiment" in Moscow, and eagerly reporting their enthusiasm in the leading journals of left-leaning opinion.

Writing a highly touted series in 1928 for *The New Republic*, John Dewey, godfather and icon of modern public education, raved about the "progress" he discovered in the "great experiment" in Bolshevik Russia, which he deemed a "great success." The Columbia professor had voyaged there that summer, along with 25 American educators from various universities. There, the breathless progressives were paraded from Potemkin village to Potemkin village. The objective of the hospitable Bolshevik government was to dupe these influential American intellectuals into favorable impressions that they would not only write about back home (in leading publications), but also to enlist them in a campaign to pressure the U.S. government into officially recognizing Stalin's totalitarian state. Excitedly recording his glowing impressions for *The New Republic*, Dewey did just that, filing an extremely influential six-part series that ran from November 14, 1928 through December 19, 1928.[6]

Dewey's outrageous reporting in that series is too vast to summarize in a few passages here, but among the gems: the professor praised the "orderly and safe character of life in Russia."[7] Of course, Dewey made certain exceptions: "In spite of secret police, inquisitions, arrests and deportations of Nepmen and Kulaks, exiling of party opponents, including divergent elements in the party, life for the masses goes on with regularity, safety and decorum."[8]

Dewey concluded his series for *The New Republic* by doing precisely what his Soviet handlers had hoped he would. He insisted upon "political recognition of Russia on the part of the United States." The professor-turned-journalist conceded that his trip had brought him to that conclusion: "I went to Russia with no conviction on that subject.... I came away with the feeling that the maintenance of barriers that prevent intercourse, knowledge and understanding is close to a crime against humanity."[9]

In other words, Stalin's minions had changed the professor's mind.

The duping was complete – *a great success by the great experiment*.

The New Republic to this day remains one of the top journals of American leftist opinion. Joining Dewey at *The New Republic* was another stalwart progressive champion, Lincoln Steffens. "I am a patriot for Russia," the popular journalist proudly proclaimed. "The Future is there; Russia will win out and it will save the world."[10]

Perhaps even more respected than Steffens was

Upton Sinclair. For the left, this journalist, writer, and novelist extraordinaire, was no less than a beacon of moral truth, a crusader for the common man. Unfortunately, he was also a dependable dupe for his communist friends. As a case in point, Sinclair was taken hook, line, and sinker by one of the worst communist front-groups, Friends of the Soviet Union, which (unbeknownst to liberals/progressives) had been created by the American Communist Party in the early 1920s. Initially called "Friends of Soviet Russia," the Comintern in 1929 directed the group to make a slight name change – in addition to ordering it to defend the Soviet Union and explicitly push for U.S. recognition of Stalin's regime.[11]

Friends of the Soviet Union published a propaganda organ called *Soviet Russia Today*. It was controlled by well-known communists such as William Z. Foster – CPUSA head and an ACLU board member – Anna Louise Strong, Karl Radek, Maxim Gorky, and Theodore Dreiser. Among them, Foster openly advocated a "Soviet American Republic" as part of a "world Soviet Union."[12] Despite these dubious characters, the usually cynical Sinclair was game. He offered himself up. Enlisted among the contributing editors to *Soviet Russia Today* was the great moral conscience of progressive journalism: Upton Sinclair. Sinclair provided a photo for the inside of the magazine next to a dutiful quote that affirmed: "Will do my part to expose the lies and slanders against Soviet Russia. Your publication will bring the true facts to light."[13]

Sinclair's promise came directly above those of William Z. Foster and Anna Louise Strong, a horrible Soviet propagandist. Strong's and Foster's Soviet sympathies were patently transparent. Upton Sinclair was a progressive dupe for their cause.

And then there was the now notorious Walter Duranty, another exhibit from the *New York Times*.[14] Few Western reporters so unwaveringly served the Soviet line in the 1930s, especially via his unforgivably misleading reporting on the catastrophic famine in the Ukraine in the 1930s. Duranty's work stunned his contemporaries, even the left-leaning among them. One such observer was Eugene Lyons, who, as a young man in New York, had joined the Young People's Socialist League even before he arrived at the communist hotbed that was Columbia University. Lyons later lost his admiration for the USSR after living there for several years as a UPI correspondent. He noticed, however, that Duranty's admiration never waned. In his 1941 classic, *The Red Decade*, Lyons wrote that Duranty took an "angle" in his reporting that was "true-blue Stalinist."[15]

That was also the interpretation of another erstwhile man of the left, the famed British reporter-pundit Malcolm Muggeridge, whose observances of the incredible gullibility of Western progressives in Stalin's Russia shocked him so much that it was a powerful factor repelling him from political left altogether. "The almost unbelievable credulity of these mostly university-educated tourists," wrote Muggeridge, "astonished even Soviet officials used to handling foreign visitors."[16]

Among the most astonishing was Walter Duranty, who, said Muggeridge, wrote "everything the Soviet authorities wanted him to – that collectivization of agriculture was working well, with no famine conditions anywhere; that the purges were justified, the confessions genuine, and the judicial procedure impeccable."[17] That was bad enough. But making it worse, "The *New York Times* went on all those years giving great prominence to Duranty's messages, building him and them up when they were so evidently nonsensically untrue." According to Muggeridge, the *Times* did this "to the point that he came to be accepted as the great Russian expert in America, and played a major part in shaping President Roosevelt's policies vis-à-vis the USSR."[18]

For such reporting, Duranty would receive no less

than a Pulitzer (1932). In an ironic way, this set the standard for journalistic dupery. As Muggeridge agreed, "Since [Duranty's] time, there have been a whole succession of others fulfilling this same role – in Cuba, in Vietnam, in Latin America."[19]

Another in that line of succession was I. F. Stone, a leading light for the enlightened American left, celebrated by liberals for decades as the "conscience" of journalism, as a hero, as a liberal "saint."[20] The latest archival research, however, suggests that Stone was (for a time) a paid Soviet agent. In their latest work, published by Yale University Press, historians John Earl Haynes, Harvey Klehr, and Alexander Vassiliev flatly conclude that Stone was a "Soviet spy."[21] The great authority on communism and the Venona papers, the late Herb Romerstein, concluded: "it is clear from the evidence that Stone was indeed a Soviet agent."[22] A likewise strong testimony comes from Oleg Kalugin, the aforementioned *New York Times'* Russian "personality kid." "He [Stone] was a KGB agent since 1938," states Kalugin. "His code name was 'Blin.' When I resumed relations with him in 1966, it was on Moscow's instructions. Stone was a devoted Communist."[23]

If Stone did indeed eventually leave the Soviet side, which he seems to have done (as Kalugin himself maintains), he remained on the left as a liberal/progressive, where he would frequently continue to play sucker to communist ambitions. And yet after all of this, Stone would forever remain a darling of the liberal media. A "journalist" of their own making and desiring.

Finally, another prominent example of duping was the case of Drew Pearson, the extremely influential syndicated columnist from the 1940s through the 1960s. Pearson reveled in attacking leading anticommunists of his day, especially Joe McCarthy. This tendency was encouraged by at least two top staffers to Pearson who were closet CPUSA supporters if not outright members. One of them was David Karr, formerly of the *Daily Worker* and apparently (according to archival information) a KGB source. Among other fascinating roles, Karr in the 1970s served as the link between the Kremlin and senators John Tunney and Ted Kennedy (mentioned later in this report) – long after he dutifully served Drew Pearson, America's most widely read columnist.[24]

This penchant to be duped, sadly too common to many liberal/progressive journalists, continued from the 1920s through the 1980s, the final decade of the Cold War. As to the latter period, the roster of liberal reporters blasting Ronald Reagan's anti-Soviet efforts in the 1980s was deep: Mary McGrory, James "Scotty" Reston (again, the *New York Times*), Helen Thomas, Dan Rather, Bill Moyers, TV journalist Phil Donahue, and many, many more. *New York Times*' columnist Anthony Lewis called Reagan's "Evil Empire" remarks – an absolutely accurate charge that no one in the Soviet Union would dispute – "outrageous." More than that, said Lewis, they were "dangerous," "sectarian," "simplistic," and "primitive – the only word for it."[25]

Lewis's language no doubt thrilled the Kremlin, which was apoplectic over the impact and undeniable truth of Reagan's remarks.

In truth, it was not unusual for the Kremlin to seize remarks like those of Lewis or other American journalists and thrust them onto the front page of *Pravda* or recycle them as a means to attack Reagan. For instance, an October 8, 1985 attack piece on Reagan by *New York Times* editorialist Karl Meyer – which wrongly accused Reagan of incorrectly quoting Lenin – was directly picked up and used against Reagan by Soviet propagandists Georgi Arbatov and Valentin Falin.[26] Likewise, a November 1, 1983 *Washington Post* op-ed by editor Robert Kaiser, which blasted the Reagan administration's invasion of Grenada, was essentially turned into a TASS press release disseminated throughout the Soviet empire.[27]

It is no exaggeration at all to say that the Kremlin adored these anti-Reagan screeds by top American journalists, and found them highly useful. These journalists were, in effect, serving as what Vladimir Lenin called "useful idiots."

Examples such as this could be cited by the boatload, akin to the boatloads of Potemkin progressives and political pilgrims who made the voyage to the Soviet Motherland, confident that they had discovered the Brave New World. Again, however, this mere one report could not begin to house them all. Instead, this report will examine a handful of added examples, moving chronologically from earliest to present day, and dealing with dupes misled by communists worldwide – not just in Moscow. We will stop first in China, with a look at the work of Edgar Snow, whose remarkably bad reportage on Mao Tse-tung has been forgotten by historians. After Snow, we will consider Herb Matthews' terribly destructive *New York Times'* dispatches on Fidel Castro, and how his sins have been replicated by journalists covering Cuba still today. Beyond Cuba and China, we will look at the liberal media's most heralded news anchor of his generation, Walter Cronkite, and also at Curtis MacDougall, a hard-left journalist (with many communist associations) who trained numerous liberal journalists with his popular textbook, *Interpretative Reporting*. Finally, we will wrap up with an examination of Frank Marshall Davis, Barack Obama's mentor, and how his dedicated work for the communist cause has been blacklisted by modern journalists whose first duty is to protect and advance their president: Barack Obama.

Chapter 3
Edgar Snow's *Red Star*

Among the most forgotten of left-leaning journalists who helped the cause of international communism was Edgar Snow (1905-72). With Snow, it was the communist cause in China that was aided and abetted.

Snow might have seemed an unlikely candidate to serve as a dupe to Mao Tse-tung. He wrote not for the *New York Times* or *The New Republic* but for the more conservative, popularly minded, and anti-communist *Saturday Evening Post*. Nonetheless, his *Red Star Over China* (first published in 1938) became what Cold War historians M. Stanton Evans and Herb Romerstein called "an unabashed commercial on behalf of the communist Mao Tse-tung and his Yenan comrades."[28]

To be sure, Snow's book was a major work, deserved to be taken seriously. Before its writing, Snow had already lived in China for seven years, lecturing at universities and doing stories for major newspapers such as the *Chicago Tribune*, the *New York Sun*, the *New York Herald Tribune*, and *London Daily Herald*. Over 540 pages in length and highly acclaimed by the journalistic elite – including fellow journalist and China observer John King Fairbank – Snow's account was packed with primary sources and intimate details, including multiple lengthy first-person interviews with Mao himself. He had access few to no other journalists had. In total, he generated 20,000 words worth of interviews with Mao. The problem is that he accepted much of this uncritically, whereas he was anything but uncritical of Mao's opponents: Chiang Kai-Shek and his nationalists. His four-hour talk with Mao in 1965, which was used in a later (1968) edition of the book, was the first full-length interview Mao had given to any reporter in six years. And when one considers the content of Snow's words on Mao, it is no surprise that the chairman was happy to give the American journalist an exclusive.[29]

Fittingly, Mao was among those to whom Snow gave thanks in the opening of the 1968 edition, which was released smack in the middle of the horrific Cultural Revolution, a bloody evil that Snow benignly called a "thoroughgoing social revolution." That was a definite euphemism, as was Snow's repeatedly misguided use of the phrase "democracy" in describing Mao's doings.[30]

Today, Mao is recognized for the mass killer that he was. But Edgar Snow did not see him that way. Snow described Mao as a "rather Lincolnesque figure ... with large, searching eyes." Those eyes bespoke an "intellectual face of great shrewdness." He portrayed Mao as a common man, an everyman. The first time that Snow saw Mao, he was struck, if not hooked. According to Snow, the chairman was walking along talking to two young peasants, "gesticulating earnestly," moving along "unconcernedly," even as the diabolical Chiang had placed a $250,000 bounty on his head. Here was the everyman with the common man. "The story of Mao's life was a rich cross-section of a whole generation [of Chinese]," recorded Snow. "There would never be any one 'savior' of China, yet undeniably one felt a certain force of destiny in Mao."[31]

Snow was certain that this romantic figure could become "a very great man." This certainty sprung from the "uncanny degree" to which Mao "synthesized and expressed the urgent demands of millions of Chinese, especially the peasantry." According to Snow, "everyone knew and respected" Mao. Snow personally said that he had "never met anyone who did not like" or "admire" Mao. This was because the Chinese communist leader had a "deep sense of personal dignity," and appeared "quite free from symptoms of megalomania." He was an "ardent student of philosophy" and insatiably interested in and curious about international events and foreign affairs. According to Snow, who admired Franklin Roosevelt, Mao saw FDR as a man that Red China "could cooperate with." The chairman was especially intrigued by the New Deal.[32]

The youthful Mao, said Snow, had harbored "strongly liberal and humanistic tendencies," and was still "a humanist in a fundamental sense." Snow figured that Mao had probably been a "moderating influence" within the communist movement. He had also reportedly carried over from his youth an intense work ethic, an "iron constitution." He could withstand "great hardship and suffering." He combined the "personal habits" of a peasant with an "extraordinary mind." Overall, said Snow, "Mao impressed me as a man of considerable depth of feeling. I remember that his eyes moistened once or twice when he was speaking of dead comrades." In fact, it was typical of the benevolent Mao to hand his coat to a wounded man at the front.[33]

Snow consistently expressed such sentiments as he waxed poetically of the Red Chinese, whom he framed as anti-imperialist, anti-fascist, and even (at times) Christian. They wanted to educate people, these "Red companions" did. They were sunny, jovial chaps, and their territory and countryside was nothing short of tranquil, beautiful, idyllic. Snow spent time with them, hunting, fishing, smoking, laughing – at peace. They were one with themselves and nature. They put Snow quickly at ease. Chiang and his forces, on the other hand, were downright repressive; they were bandits, brigands, kidnappers, killers, fascists, dictators, cretins. They made Snow feel much less safe. The Reds, on the other hand, simply wanted to "stop civil war," and, in fact, were so genuinely kind and good-hearted that only they, it seemed, could be so giving, so caring as to spare Chiang's life. If Chiang ever desired to see compassion, he might look to the poor yet benign communist souls that he and his ilk had tormented for so long.[34]

The effect of Snow's tome was significant. It was translated and reprinted in multiple editions, and, of course, did not hurt the communist cause in China. In October 1949, Mao and friends prevailed, turning the most populated country in the world communist. Was the result peace and harmony and justice and tranquility? Hardly.

The immediate casualties were all basic rights and civil liberties in China: property, speech, press, assembly, religion, and even the pursuit of happiness. The private life was banned entirely. Everything was pooled together and collectivized, from pots and pans and woks to the collective smoke that was the only smoke permitted to emanate from the collective kitchen. Within just two decades, after Mao's Long March (1957-60) and Cultural Revolution (1966-69), tens of millions were dead. *The Black Book of Communism*, the seminal Harvard University Press work, estimated upwards of 65 million deaths in China due to communism, making it (and Mao) the largest killer of any people in any country in all of human history. Even then, those estimates might be low: The latest research, including that published by Jung Chang and Jon Halliday, projects that Mao might have killed over 70 million.[35]

And even worse, those numbers do not do justice to the total slaughter. Mao's "Sinification of Marxism" ushered the communist ideology into wider Asia, where emulators would destroy yet more lives in places like Korea, Vietnam – both of which involved America going to war and losing almost 100,000 boys – and Cambodia. In Cambodia, Pol Pot's Khmer Rouge killed upwards of 2-3 million out of a population of 5-7 million in just four years (1975-79).

Despite Edgar Snow's rosy reports, Mao and what he offered was not sunny and promising. It was dark and deadly. There was no peace and "personal dignity" in anything that Mao Tse-tung brought to China. This was no "great man" and most assuredly no "savior."

Chapter 4

Herb Matthews: The *New York Times'* Man in Havana

While Snow's work boosted communists in China, another reporter served as a booster for communists in America's backyard: Cuba.

Herbert L. Matthews (1900-1977) was a *New York Times* reporter and editorial writer, and it was often difficult for readers to discern the difference in the two. A graduate of Columbia University, Matthews' bias and sympathy for communist causes was first evident in his dispatches from Spain during the Spanish Civil War, leaving many to wonder whether Matthews was pro-communist, a communist himself, a fellow traveler, or a duped liberal/progressive. To that end, he followed closely in the footsteps of earlier *Times* reporter Walter Duranty, who was very much his forerunner.

Matthews' liberal supporters insist he was one of them. Interestingly, others who also saw Matthews on their side were Fidel Castro and friends. Matthews' extraordinarily influential reports from Cuba in 1957 breathed entirely new life into Fidel's movement, which the world had given up for dead. Later, Che Guevara himself would contend, "When the world had given us up for dead, the interview with Matthews put the lie to our disappearance."[36]

In short, Herb Matthews' reportage at the *Times* provides another example of the liberal media yet again changing the course of history in favor of America's adversaries. This time, it was in favor of a totalitarian Cuba, one that five years later would host Soviet nuclear missiles aimed at the United States.

Matthews' page-one, three-part series on Castro first appeared in the *New York Times* on February 24, 1957. It was a blockbuster.[37]

Fidel Castro had launched his revolution on July 26, 1953, but it had languished at best. It was, by all accounts, on the run and effectively finished. International support and enthusiasm had correspondingly waned. But Castro's fortunes were about to change, courtesy of the *New York Times*.

Matthews began his game-changer of a story by reporting that Castro, "the rebel leader of Cuba's youth," was, in fact, "alive and fighting hard and successfully in the rugged, almost impenetrable fastnesses of the Sierra Maestra." He was doing so against all odds, claimed Matthews, and in the face of Fulgencio Batista throwing everything at him: "President Fulgencio Batista has the cream of his Army around the area, but the Army men are fighting a thus-far losing battle to destroy the most dangerous enemy General Batista has yet faced in a long and adventurous career as a Cuban leader and dictator."[38]

Matthews then touted his scoop: "This is the first sure news that Fidel Castro is still alive and still in Cuba. No one connected with the outside world, let alone with the press, has seen Senor Castro except this writer. No one in Havana, not even at the United States Embassy with its resources for getting information, will know until this report is published that Fidel Castro is really in the Sierra Maestra."

Matthews seemed to celebrate a personal achievement against Batista, much like Edgar Snow extolling Mao's survival against Chiang Kai-Shek and Chiang's "corrupt" nationalists. Matthews said of his story: "This account, among other things, will break the tightest censorship in the history of the Cuban Republic ... Havana does not and cannot know that thousands of men and women are heart and soul with

Fidel Castro and the new deal for which they think he stands."

Note that loaded word for the *New York Times* faithful: "new deal." Castro, FDR-like, was offering Cubans a "new deal." Like Edgar Snow's Mao, Castro was likewise framed as having FDR-like pretenses, a kind of a new dealer – and a democrat. Matthews wrote:

> Fidel Castro and his 26th of July Movement are the flaming symbol of this opposition to the [Batista] regime. The organization, which is apart from the university students' opposition, is formed of youths of all kinds. It is a revolutionary movement that calls itself socialistic. It is also nationalistic, which generally in Latin America means anti-Yankee. The program is vague and couched in generalities, but it amounts to a new deal for Cuba, radical, democratic and therefore anti-Communist. The real core of its strength is that it is fighting against the military dictatorship of President Batista.

By Herb Matthews' narrative, the bad guy in this equation was Fulgencio Batista, not Fidel Castro. Just like Snow's China, the true "democrat" was the communist – except here, in Matthews' telling, Castro was more than that. Castro was an "anti-Communist." Such was how Herb Matthews opened his apologia for the man who would become the Western Hemisphere's longest running communist dictator ever. And Matthews was not finished. He went on to frame Fidel as not just a democrat and anti-communist, but a constitutionalist, a beacon of liberty, an advocate of freedom and free elections, an anti-colonialist, an anti-imperialist, a champion of social justice ... and an extraordinarily eloquent one at that:

> Senor Castro speaks some English, but he preferred to talk in Spanish, which he did

with extraordinary eloquence. His is a political mind rather than a military one. He has strong ideas of liberty, democracy, social justice, the need to restore the Constitution, to hold elections. He has strong ideas on economy, too, but an economist would consider them weak.

The 26th of July Movement talks of nationalism, anti-colonialism, anti-imperialism. I asked Senor Castro about that. He answered, "You can be sure we have no animosity toward the United States and the American people."

"Above all," he said, "we are fighting for a democratic Cuba and an end to the dictatorship. We are not anti-military; that is why we let the soldier prisoners go. There is no hatred of the Army as such, for we know the men are good and so are many of the officers." [...]

"Why should soldiers die for Batista for $72 a month?" he asked. "When we win, we will give them $100 a month, and they will serve a free, democratic Cuba."

Ah, yes – *a free and democratic Cuba*. Much like the free and democratic China that Mao created.

Matthews' article was a masterpiece for the communist cause. It is no exaggeration to say that the *Daily Worker* itself could not have produced such a perfect piece of political propaganda to dupe the masses. After all, such a piece would not have been believable in the *Daily Worker*, but the *Times* was the *Times* – daily bread for the liberal/progressive masses. The only remaining question was whether Herb Matthews was assuming the role of dupe or doing the duping himself. But this much we know: the impact of his article was huge for Castro, and a major blow to the efforts of anti-communists who wanted to save their island from a man who would soon take all their property and most basic civil liberties.

As was later joked about by conservatives, quite uneasily, Castro had arguably gotten his job through the *New York Times*. The importance of Matthews' article cannot be understated.

Once Castro had been rescued by the *Times*, and shot his way into power in Havana in January 1959, he came to New York City for a victory lap, where CPUSA and the *Daily Worker* turned out massive crowds wherever they could. There, the duping of a wider net of wide-eyed liberals/progressives continued with great alacrity.

Among the easily taken was writer Norman Mailer, who got goose-bumps at the sight of Fidel: "So Fidel Castro, I announce to the City of New York that you gave all of us who are alone in this country ... some sense that there were heroes in the world. One felt life in one's overargued blood as one picked up in our newspaper the details of your voyage." What sort of voyage? According to Mailer, "It was as if the ghost of Cortez had appeared in our century riding Zapata's white horse. You were the first and greatest hero to appear in the world since the Second War."[39]

Mailer's swooning over Castro was outdone perhaps only by I. F. Stone's crush on Castro's comrade, Che Guevara. "He was the first man I had ever met whom I thought not just handsome but beautiful," wrote Stone of his beloved Che. "With his curly, reddish beard, he looked like a cross between a faun and a Sunday school print of Jesus.... In a sense he was, like some early saint, taking refuge in the desert."[40]

It might be more comforting to say that such ridiculous adulation by the likes of Mailer and Stone and Herb Matthews ended in the 1950s, but that sadly isn't the case. Today's journalists have not done a much better job covering Castro's Cuba. They regularly rave about Cuba's array of "free" services, from education to healthcare – as if these things cost nothing to anyone or anything, as if the money grows like sugar cane, there for the harvesting.

"Medical care ... is available to every Cuban and it is free," reported Peter Jennings, ABC's longtime news anchor, in 1989, as communism was dying in the Soviet Bloc but being pushed with renewed vigor in Cuba. "Some of Cuba's healthcare is world class. In heart disease, for example, in brain surgery. Health and education are the revolution's great success stories."[41]

It is inexplicable how or why Jennings would have pointed to Cuban "brain surgery" as a so-called success story. Rather, Cuba under Castro has been rightly condemned for doing lobotomies, not to mention locking up homosexuals in mental institutions. For some reason, though, Jennings was told to hail Cuba's "world class" "brain surgery." Perhaps because it is government provided, which, to many liberals, makes it "free."

Peter Jennings was not alone in his naïveté. "The level of public services was remarkable!" marveled reporter Maria Shriver of the "Today" show during a managed tour of Havana conducted by Fidel's handlers. "Free education, medicine, and heavily subsidized housing."[42]

Shriver's NBC colleague Ed Rabel was likewise impressed: "There is, in Cuba, government intrusion into everyone's life, from the moment he is born until the day he dies." For Rabel, this was meant as a positive – a giant positive: "The reasoning is that the government wants to better the lives of its citizens and keep them from exploiting or hurting one another.... On a sunny day in a park in the old city of Havana it is difficult to see anything that is sinister."[43]

In fact, it is difficult to see a lot of things in Cuba. In addition to the lack of commerce, property rights, and freedom of speech and press and assembly and religion and conscience and travel and emigration and the right to open a business or grow a private garden plot or criticize the Castro regime, one also sees no boats. In a surreal spectacle, Cuba is an island without boats.

Boats have been seized by the government; if they were not, people would use them not for fishing or recreation but to flee the island. Because they have no boats, untold numbers of repressed citizens have attempted the treacherous 100-mile swim to Florida in shark-infested waters. It is estimated that some 100,000 have risked the journey, with perhaps as many as 30,000 to 40,000 drowning. As they bob for breath, the government employs the resources of the state to literally strike them, dropping large bags of sand on top of them from helicopters hovering high above.[44]

Aside from these embattled souls, how many additional people has Fidel Castro killed since coming to power? The numbers vary, but the typical estimated total is between 10,000 and 20,000, whether victims of long-term imprisonment or outright execution by bullets to the head. Most credible estimates place the total somewhere between 15,000 to 17,000 dead, which, for the record, would be five to six times the number of dead credited to Chile's "right-wing dictator" Augusto Pinochet, whom leftists hounded for decades as a war criminal meriting immediate prosecution – totally contrary to the left's adulation for Castro.

None of these stubborn facts, however, have dampened liberal journalists' love for all that miraculous "free" stuff that everyday Cubans allegedly desire so much – in the expert opinion of American reporters (not to mention left-wing documentarians like Michael Moore and Oliver Stone).

Speaking of love, the passions burn deep for Castro's Cuba at CNN, from its founder, Ted Turner, who called Castro "one hell of a guy," and has spent many hours smoking cigars with the dictator, to the reporters at CNN's "Newsroom." As to the latter, Morgan Neil did an August 2009 "special edition" on location from one of Fidel's Havana hospitals – a hospital that Neil was permitted to see in one of the dictator's Potemkin villages. "Impressive statistics!" said Neil, accepting the information that the totalitarian regime served up.

"Cuba's infant mortality rates are the lowest in the hemisphere, in line with those of Canada!"[45]

Agreeing with Neil is Katie Couric, who, after praising Cuba's "terrific healthcare system," commended the communist country's standard of living, which, she reported, is "very high for a Third World country." *Washington Post* reporter Don Podesta agreed, claiming that Cuba "has eliminated abject need," particularly thanks to its "education and medical care."[46]

There has been no shortage of duped reporters who have admired Fidel Castro's prison state for decades.[47] Herb Matthews started something alright – more than he could have ever imagined.

Chapter 5

And That's the Way It Isn't: Walter Cronkite's World

Walter Cronkite (1916-2009) was heralded by his liberal media colleagues as "the most trusted man in America." He was *America's anchorman*, a seat he held at CBS News for nearly 20 years from the early 1960s to the early 1980s, when he was replaced by an anchor even more transparently biased – Dan Rather. Cronkite claimed he was not biased in his reporting, or at least that he did his best to prevent bias from infecting his reporting.

Americans became bitterly divided over Cronkite's work on the Vietnam War. When Walter Cronkite turned against the war, so did his reporting and so did much of America. His insistence that the Tet offensive was an American "defeat" was particularly detrimental to U.S. efforts. An analysis by Ernest Lefever concluded that of 1,479 "CBS Evening News" reports on the war, 1,400 supported the anti-war or "dovish" perspective. Accuracy in Media founder Reed Irvine expressed a not-uncommon belief that Cronkite "contributed a great deal to our defeat in Vietnam."[48]

Nonetheless, Cronkite tried to conceal his left-leaning views from the public, including his odd admiration for global governance, which (once no longer at CBS) he openly professed during a candid speech to the World Federalist Association, a group that advocates not only a single world government but global taxes by Americans to pay for their new international regime. In 1999, Cronkite was honored with the group's coveted Norman Cousins Global Governance Award, hailing him as a "lifelong advocate" of global government.[49] "The proud nations someday will see the light," prophesied Cronkite hopefully, speaking of America and all nations of the world. They will someday seek a "system of world order" and "yield up their precious sovereignty, just as America's thirteen colonies did two centuries ago."[50]

In Cronkite's estimation, it was time for a new Founding, a new American revolution. This one would cede the Founders' sovereignty to the dictates of a global regime.

Like many liberals, Walter Cronkite was unsettled by the election of Ronald Reagan in November 1980. He was no doubt eager to confront Reagan, and was prompted by the new president's first press conference on January 29, 1981. This was an unforgettable debut by Reagan, making clear that Jimmy Carter had indeed left the White House. When the new president was asked about Soviet aims and intentions, he calmly explained to the Washington press corps that the Soviet leadership had "openly and publicly declared that the only morality they recognize is what will further their cause, meaning they reserve unto themselves the right to commit any crime, to lie, to cheat...." Reagan insisted this was consistent with what Soviet founder, Vladimir Lenin, had preached.

The new president could not have been more clear and confident, and liberal journalists could not have been more upset and offended. They figured that the addled old right-wing actor must have read this Lenin stuff from some fictionalized script in Hollywood or some sloppy *Readers Digest* round-up.

And so, they (and the Soviets) were surely thrilled when the venerable Walter Cronkite called out the bomb-throwing rookie president. CBS's feted newsman got his chance during a March 3 one-on-one with the White House's new uncompromising anti-communist. Suggesting that he was speaking for others (and not himself), Cronkite told Reagan that "there are some who ... feel that you might have overdone the rhetoric a little bit in laying into the Soviet leadership as being liars and thieves, et cetera." The new president's views apparently struck *some people* (but not necessarily Cronkite, presumably) as too "hard line toward the Soviet Union."[51]

Reagan, for the record, was not rattled. He smiled and gently corrected these unnamed "some people." "Well, now, let's recap," said Reagan. He explained to the CBS news anchor that he had simply responded honestly to a journalist's question about "Soviet aims." "I don't have to offer my opinion," Reagan told Cronkite. "They [the Soviets] have told us where they're going again and again. They have told us their goal is the Marxian philosophy of world revolution and a single, one-world communist state, and that they're dedicated to that."

Reagan was not offering opinion but fact. He told the old reporter that this old president was simply reporting the truth the way it is. "Remember," Reagan said of the Soviets, warning Cronkite not to be "naïve," "their ideology is without God, without our idea of morality in a religious sense." He doubled down on his press conference assessment, again insisted that the Soviets "resort to lying or stealing or cheating or even murder if it furthers their cause.... [W]e have to keep that in mind when we deal with them."

Cronkite, however, seemed un-assuaged, perturbed, bothered. This was not what he wanted to hear.

Another Reagan-related incident with the Soviets would no doubt have intrigued Cronkite; it was a fascinating way in which his name was personally connected with Reagan and the Soviet leadership – namely, in a May 14, 1983 document written by Soviet KGB head Victor Chebrikov to Soviet leader Yuri Andropov.[52] (*See* Appendix, Figure 2.)

This remarkable memo to General Secretary Andropov was sent with "Special Importance" under the highest classification. The subject line stated: "Regarding Senator Kennedy's request to the General Secretary of the Communist Party Y. V. Andropov." It concerned a "confidential" offer to Andropov from Senator Ted Kennedy (D-Mass.).

What sort of offer?

According to the memo, Kennedy was "very troubled." It was the souring of US-Soviet relations that disturbed the Massachusetts senator, and especially because the souring was the result not of the Kremlin and Yuri Andropov, according to Kennedy – to the contrary, Kennedy said he was "very impressed" with Andropov – but Reagan, of whom Kennedy was not impressed. The worsening of relations was, in Kennedy's opinion, due to "Reagan's belligerence," especially his defense policies. "According to Kennedy," reported Chebrikov, "the current threat is due to the President's refusal to engage any modification to his politics." Worse still, that stubbornness was (allegedly) calcified by Reagan's unfortunate political success, which, stated Kennedy, made Reagan even more confident of his success and policies, and also more re-electable. The latter may have been Kennedy's chief concern: the 1984 election was only a year away, and Reagan seemed eminently re-electable. Kennedy was considering a run.

What to do about this Reagan problem?

Chebrikov's memo eagerly zeroed in on the heart of Kennedy's proposal: The KGB head reported that Kennedy had identified a glimmer of hope as to where Reagan's policies and reelection bid might be stopped. The president might well be vulnerable, even with his admitted popularity and political success. The senior senator from Massachusetts had identified a possible chink in Reagan's political armor. As Chebrikov put it, "The only real threats to Reagan are problems of war and peace and Soviet-American relations. These issues, according to the senator [Kennedy], will without a doubt become the most important of the election campaign."

Alas, then, the KGB head relayed Kennedy's proposal to the head of the Soviet Union: "Kennedy believes that, given the state of current affairs, and in the interest of peace, it would be prudent and timely to undertake the following steps to counter the militaristic politics of Reagan."

This was where the media could help; that is, the liberal media – American journalists who might he hoodwinked into aiding our adversaries. Kennedy identified two steps to counter Reagan, the second of which involved "the most trusted man in America." The first step, according to Ted Kennedy's plan, was for Andropov to invite the Massachusetts senator to Moscow for a personal meeting. As Chebrikov explained it, "The main purpose of the meeting, according to the senator, would be to arm Soviet officials with explanations regarding problems of nuclear disarmament so they would be better prepared and more convincing during appearances in the USA."

The second step, said the KGB head, was a Kennedy scheme to help the Soviets "influence Americans." Kennedy even had ideas as to who these agents of influence might be. Said Chebrikov: "Kennedy believes that in order to influence Americans it would be important to organize in August-September of this year [1983], televised interviews with Y. V. Andropov in the USA." Kennedy hoped that this would assist the Soviet dictator in conducting a "direct appeal" to the American people.

So far, so good. Who would do these important TV interviews? Who would arrange them?

"Kennedy and his friends," explained the head of the KGB, had ideas. Here, Kennedy singled out Walter Cronkite as an ideal candidate for sit-down interviews with the dictator. Perhaps Cronkite might even come to Moscow. As the memo stated: "Specifically, the president of the board of directors of ABC, Elton Raul, and television columnists Walter Cronkite or Barbara Walters could visit Moscow."

Recruiting Cronkite hardly seemed a long shot. Liberals and Soviet officials alike watched him come around to their view on the Vietnam War in the 1970s. So, why would he not share their view on Reagan and the Cold War in the 1980s? In fact, they understood that he indeed shared their view on Reagan and the Cold War. After Cronkite had left the news-desk in 1981, the well-known partisan Democrat had not been shy about publicly criticizing Reagan's Soviet policy, defense policies, military build-up, nuclear strategy, military intervention in Grenada in 1983 and Libya in 1986, and more.[53]

Whatever became of Kennedy's offer? We do not know. No one in the liberal media ever bothered to push Kennedy for an answer, nor Cronkite – even as the remarkable 1983 memo was declassified and first discovered by a BBC reporter, Tim Sebastian. Sebastian broke the story in the *London Times* in February 1992, which was never followed up or covered in the mainstream American media.[54] The *New York Times* and *Washington Post* and allies were not interested. The entirety of the mainstream media ignored the story and let Kennedy off the hook.[55] Kennedy took the details of his offer to the grave. And we also never heard from Walter Cronkite on the senator's generous offer to serve up the former CBS anchor as a conduit for the Soviet dictator.

For the record, also not interviewed about this stunning story was the liaison between Kennedy and the KGB: former California Democratic Senator John Tunney. Tunney was an old law school pal of Kennedy. Tunney is still alive today. Not alive is a third figure who acted as a liaison between Kennedy and Tunney and the Soviets: David Karr. Karr, recall, had been the pro-communist staff member to Drew Pearson decades earlier, and a KGB source. Karr died in 1979.

Finally, we also never learned of Walter Cronkite's reaction to another Cold War development, this one disclosed in a document declassified from archives not long after his death. In May 2010, Cliff Kincaid broke an intriguing revelation mined from a June 25, 1986 document that he procured via a Freedom of Information Act request. The document was addressed to the FBI director and to the attention of the bureau's intelligence division. Originally classified "secret," with some names still redacted, the FBI document shows how communists targeted Cronkite and four other journalists, including Bill Moyers and Phil Donahue, as a possible candidate to sign and endorse the so-called "People's Peace Treaty." This was a pro-Soviet and Soviet-led "treaty" that aimed to rally certain high-profile American leftists from various professions and walks of life: the scientific community, artists, labor, clergy, and (among others) media. The largest space on the document was the space set aside for media recruits. Liberal journalists were apparently viewed as the largest category for potential useful idiots. (*See* Appendix, Figure 3.)

The organizers looked to assemble a 13-member delegation for the "treaty" signing ceremony. It was hoped that Cronkite might be one of them. He was among those that organizers endeavored to "seek out."

The effort was part of a Soviet "active measures" campaign aimed at undermining President Reagan's foreign policy, and specifically his defense policies intended to bring the Soviets to the negotiating table and challenge them to an arms race they could not afford and would bankrupt themselves if they tried. The Soviets saw Cronkite as potentially useful.

This Kremlin-based propaganda campaign was coordinated with the communist front-group the National Council of American-Soviet Friendship, founded by CPUSA way back in 1943 as a reincarnated version of Friends of the Soviet Union – which, as noted earlier, had suckered the likes of Upton Sinclair, and had been headed by Corliss Lamont.[56] Now, years later, the political godchildren of these old comrades were looking to enlist the likes of the "most trusted man in America," Walter Cronkite.

Much like the Ted Kennedy offer to enlist Cronkite in a scheme to help the Soviet leadership, we do not know what became of this effort. But we do know that Cronkite's past work had led communists to judge him an excellent candidate for potential exploitation. If he had seemed ripe for duping in years past, he seemed just as ripe for the present.

Chapter 6

Training "Progressive" Journalists: Curtis MacDougall

Walter Cronkite's influence on a generation of Americans and American journalists is difficult to estimate, but so was the influence of a much-less-known figure, Curtis MacDougall (1903-85).

MacDougall's impact was recently underscored in an expose by Cliff Kincaid and America's Survival.[57] As an undergraduate majoring in journalism in the 1970s, Kincaid himself had used MacDougall's book, *Interpretative Reporting*, as his college journalism textbook, and he was far from alone.[58] *Interpretative Reporting* captured MacDougall's vision for what he called "The New Journalism," an activist form of journalism that, like MacDougall's own work, would be both activist and tendentious. It would be a biased form of journalism intended to help reshape the world anew. It would be a brave and better new world, a "progressive" one.

The book was billed by the publisher, the respected MacMillan, as nothing short of a "classic" among textbooks, one that, as the publicity for the fifth edition claimed, "has led its field for more than three decades." (*See* Appendix, Figure 4.)

William David Sloan credited *Interpretative Reporting* as one of the modern "makers of the media mind."[59] As Kincaid notes, it became a standard text in journalism schools for more than 50 years. At 500-plus pages in length, the book was authoritative, as were its many claims. Among them, MacDougall listed two of the names that appear in this report, Walter Duranty and Edgar Snow, "among the best of ...journalistic scholars."[60]

But who was MacDougall, and what did he believe?

Curtis MacDougall portrayed himself as a "progressive," once even running for the U.S. Senate as the Progressive Party candidate in 1948, the year that communists nationwide rallied around Henry Wallace as their Progressive Party presidential candidate. Among his books was a three-volume history of the Progressive Party. He put his name to every "progressive" organization and cause that he could, including Progressive Citizens of America.

As MacDougall's 319-page FBI file shows,[61] however, he also put his name to numerous communist fronts or suspected front-groups, including the likes of the Abraham Lincoln School, the American Committee for Spanish Freedom, American Youth for Democracy, the Civil Rights Congress, the Chicago Committee to Secure Justice in the Rosenberg Case, the National Committee to Defeat the Mundt Bill, the Committee for Peaceful Alternatives to the Atlantic Pact, the National Committee to Abolish the House Committee on Un-American Activities, and (among many more) the National Council of American-Soviet Friendship – which, as noted in the previous section, had sought out Walter Cronkite's assistance. The FBI considered MacDougall such a potential threat that he was placed on the nation's Security Index, meaning that if a war broke out between the United States and USSR, MacDougall could have been placed under arrest. FBI documents flagged MacDougall under the headline, "Security Subjects Connected With Educational Institutions," where he was feared to be "in a position to spread Communist propaganda and wield influence over students."[62]

To liberals, however, Curtis MacDougall was a mere merry "progressive."

These activities took place mainly in the Chicago area, the host city for MacDougall's operations. There, MacDougall rubbed shoulders with Frank Marshall Davis, future mentor to the future president of the United States of America, Barack Obama. MacDougall would have met Davis in any number of communist or suspected communist-front activities. The Abraham Lincoln School, where Davis taught, would have been one of them.[63] But most notably, MacDougall and Davis would have worked together in the area of special interest to them and this report: journalism. More specifically, they would have joined forces in advancing their form of left-wing advocacy journalism.

MacDougall's name was not unfamiliar to the pages of the *Chicago Star*, the communist organ for the city of Chicago, which was founded by Frank Marshall Davis, its editor-in-chief. Among the contributors to the *Star* were a host of Communist Party USA members and, in some cases, outright Soviet agents, agents of influence, and suspects: Howard Fast, Johannes Steel, Lee Pressman, and (among others) I. F. Stone.

Frank Marshall Davis's *Star* not only worked with Curtis MacDougall but enthusiastically promoted his "progressive" candidacy for the Illinois Senate. The newspaper ran a political ad for a MacDougall appearance at a July 4, 1948 picnic celebrating the second anniversary of Davis's *Star*.[64] (*See* Appendix, Figure 5.)

This was just one of many articles in the Star touting MacDougall. In these, MacDougall showed himself no fan of either Republicans or the Democratic Party and its president, Harry Truman, the latter of who were portrayed as segregation-supporting racists who favored lynching, poll taxes, Jim Crow laws, and the general inciting of "racial hatred." MacDougall wanted the pro-Soviet Henry Wallace as American's next president and vowed to work with Wallace to advance their "progressive" agenda of "democracy."[65] (*See* Appendix, Figures 6-8.)

So intimately familiar was the *Chicago Star* to Curtis MacDougall that the "progressive" journalist joined a small group of other "progressive" journalists in purchasing the *Star* as Frank Marshall Davis left the newspaper to set sail for Hawaii, a path that would ultimately lead him into the arms of the current leader of the free world, a young, waiting Barack Obama. MacDougall and his comrades formed a group called the Progressive Publishing Company, which turned the *Star* into a "progressive" newspaper called the *Illinois Standard*. (*See* Appendix, Figure 9.)

Fittingly, then, the final issue of Frank Marshall Davis' *Star*, published September 4, 1948, included a list of the names of the stockholders, officers, and owners of the Progressive Publishing Co.[66] Among the names listed in addition to Curtis D. MacDougall were the likes of Abe Feinglass and Harry Canter. Today, a photo exists of Feinglass, a '60s war protestor long suspected by some as a potential Soviet agent of influence,[67] standing to the left of John Kerry – America's current secretary of state – as the young Kerry addressed the dubious People's Coalition for Peace & Justice Demonstration on April 24, 1971.[68] As for Harry Canter, he and his son, David, were active in Chicago left-wing politics in the 1940s. That involvement began after Harry and the family relocated to Chicago after Harry had been employed for several years in Moscow by Stalin's government as an official translator of Lenin's writings. Like Curtis MacDougall, the Canters likewise went into journalism, training future American journalists. One journalist trained by the Canter family in the 1970s was a young man named David Axelrod, the man who ultimately made Barack Obama president of the United States.[69] To bring it all full circle, just days after he successfully reelected Obama in 2012, Axelrod announced his next career ambition: training future "journalists."

Things indeed had come full circle: The Canter family mentored David Axelrod in the 1970s, training him to become a future journalist. The Canters and MacDougall had a similar vocation in that regard. So did Frank Marshall Davis, another journalist who in the 1970s mentored a young Barack Obama.

But the connections do not end with journalism. MacDougall and his comrades continued to collaborate in other forms of left-wing activism. Ironically, MacDougall and Davis, after having first worked together in Chicago's journalistic and communist circles in the 1940s, were back again working together in the 1970s – precisely the time that Davis mentored Obama. This time, the two collaborated in one of the more notorious communist fronts, the American Committee for Protection of Foreign Born (ACPFB).

This particular organization had been so radical that it had been flagged decades earlier by the Democratic Congress's seminal three-volume 1944 report, "Investigation of Un-American Propaganda Activities in the United States," which included a lengthy 15-page section strictly on ACPFB, in addition to many other references to ACPFB throughout the report.[70] As the report stated, ACPFB "was founded by the Communist Party in order to exploit racial divisions in the United States for its own revolutionary purposes."[71] In addition to this racial agitation component, ACPFB defended and sought to protect foreign communists who came to America and agitated for the Comintern, and to prevent them from deportation. One such communist was the Australian-born Harry Bridges, head of the International Longshoremen's and Warehousemen's Union (ILWU), which helped bring Frank Marshall Davis to Hawaii. The ACPFB was so clearly a tool of Soviet interests that it was designated as a subversive group by the office of President Truman's attorney general, Tom Clark, pursuant to Executive Order 10450.

As surviving documents show (*See* Appendix, Figure 10),[72] Curtis MacDougall's name appears on ACPFB letterhead from the 1970s, along with Frank

Marshall Davis and various hardcore Party members, fellow travelers, "progressives," and liberal dupes. The names range from Hugh DeLacy to Hollywood screenwriter Albert Maltz, whose Party membership was disclosed by Congress in October 1947 (Maltz's Party number was 47196).[73] DeLacy had been elected to Congress as a Democratic member from the Seattle area in the mid-1940s. He was later identified by John Abt as one of two closest CPUSA members successfully elected to Congress. The other, incidentally, was Johnny Bernard, who worked at the Abraham Lincoln School with Frank Marshall Davis and Curtis MacDougall.[74] According to Abt, DeLacy was a CPUSA member while he was a member of Congress.[75] Publicly, DeLacy referred to himself as a "progressive," as did his *New York Times* obituary.[76]

To be sure, there are many names here. It is difficult to keep track; they become confusing. They do, however, have an amazing way of coming together. And they came together in the life and mission of Curtis MacDougall.

Today, of course, liberals assure us that MacDougall was just like them: another compassionate "progressive" moving "forward" for "change." He was another happy warrior for "social justice." He was another cheerful "change agent."

In addition to writing his extremely influential textbook for college journalism majors, MacDougall would write for United Press International, the *Chicago Sun*, the *St. Louis Star-Times*, and several other newspapers and publications. He taught journalism at Northwestern University for almost 30 years.

At the time of his death in November 1987, MacDougall was working on the ninth edition of *Investigative Reporting*, eager to train another generation of journalists just like himself.[77] MacDougall's dupes today portray any suspicion of his past communist work as vile "McCarthyism," even though he was mainly investigated not by Joe McCarthy but by anti-communist Democrats who understandably feared he sided with Soviet communism. As today's liberals provide cover for Curtis MacDougall, they also further ensure that his work remains a standard for training future "progressive" reporters.

Chapter 7

Frank Marshall Davis' Press Pals

This brings us to our final subject in this report: Frank Marshall Davis. Davis was himself a journalist, one that today's liberal journalists – unwittingly serving as Davis' dupes – have been protecting in service of their primary responsibility: protecting Barack Obama.

Frank Marshall Davis (1905-87) was a pro-Soviet, pro-Red China, literal card-carrying member of the Communist Party (card/member no. 47544). Born in Kansas, he made his way to Chicago, where he joined CPUSA during World War II, and ultimately ended up in Hawaii, where he eventually met a young Obama.[78]

Davis edited and wrote for Party-line publications such as the *Chicago Star* and *Honolulu Record*, which (as noted) included contributors who served as agents to Stalin's Soviet Union. Davis did shocking Soviet propaganda work in his columns. He constantly agitated against U.S. efforts to stop Stalin's expansion into Europe and Mao's takeover of China and spread of communism into Asia. He supported the Yalta agreement because he advocated Red Army takeovers of Poland, Czechoslovakia, and all of Eastern Europe. He vilified each and every anti-communist in Europe and Asia as "fascists" undeserving of American aid. He denounced the Truman Doctrine, Marshall Plan, and Atlantic Pact, and obscenely insisted that U.S. policymakers were seeking to return the Nazis into power in West Germany, whereas the gracious and benign Stalin was seeking "democracy" in East Germany and throughout Central and Eastern Europe. He framed Truman's Marshall Plan as a new form of "colonial slavery," intended "to re-enslave the yellow and brown and black peoples of the world." He claimed that America's leaders were "aching for an excuse to launch a nuclear nightmare of mass murder and extermination" against the innocent, peace-loving Soviets and Red Chinese.[79]

Moreover, in what ought to alarm President Obama's fellow Democrats, Frank Marshall Davis's targets were chiefly Democrats, especially President Harry Truman. This was because it was Truman who stood in Stalin's way as the despot's Red Army was raping, pillaging, and rampaging through Eastern Europe. Consequently, Davis's *Chicago Star* excoriated Truman with headlines like "TRUMAN KNIFES HOPE FOR PEACE" and "White house to white hoods: KKK hails Truman's policy as its own." Davis tore into the Democratic president as trigger-happy Truman, a reckless cowboy of a president itching for "a new world war" and wildly pursuing a "program for World War III" as part of a bloodthirsty bid to "rule Russia." In Frank Marshall Davis's narrative, the threat to global peace was America and its Democratic president, not the Soviet Union and its dictator.[80]

Davis was dismissive of the Iron Curtain, as if the very thought was pure hysteria and fiction. He scoffed at Winston Churchill's courageous and prescient warning in Fulton, Missouri in March 1946. He and his comrades at CPUSA and in the *Chicago Star* mocked Churchill, insisting that the only "Iron Curtains" were those being erected by Davis's worst demons: anti-communists in the American press and General Motors. The problem was not Stalin's *Iron Curtain*, said Davis, but "G.M.'s iron curtain," being raised by "General Motors' Hitlers."[81]

More such examples could be given. In sum, they show that Frank Marshall Davis's work and writings were flatly irresponsible and outrageous.

Congress certainly noticed. In December 1956, the Democrats who headed the Senate Judiciary Committee summoned Frank Marshall Davis to Washington to testify on his pro-Soviet activities. Not surprisingly, he pled the Fifth Amendment. The extremely vocal columnist was suddenly oddly silent. The senators, however, were not fooled. The next year, the Democratic Senate, in an official report titled "Scope of Soviet Activity in the United States," publicly listed Davis as "an identified member of the Communist Party." Of this, there was no doubt.

Davis's political antics were so radical that the FBI placed him on the federal government's Security Index, which meant he could be immediately detained in the event of a national emergency, such as a war breaking out between the United States and USSR.

How and where did Barack Obama come into this picture?

Frank Marshall Davis influenced Obama throughout Obama's adolescence in the 1970s. It was Obama's grandfather, Stanley Dunham, who introduced Davis to Obama for the purpose of mentoring. In my research on Davis, I quote over a dozen biographers and associates of Obama and Davis describing Davis as a vital, lasting influence. One Davis biographer and close friend, a University of Hawaii professor, says that Davis instilled in Obama a belief that "change can happen."[82]

In fact, we first learned of Davis only because of Obama's own lengthy acknowledgment. In *Dreams from My Father*, Obama's bestselling 1995 memoir, Obama consistently referred back to his time with Davis. Obama noted that Davis offered him advice at several significant levels: on race, college, women, his mind, his attitudes, on life. "I was intrigued by old Frank," wrote Obama, "with his books and whiskey breath and the hint of hard-earned knowledge behind the hooded eyes."[83]

Obama directly mentioned "Frank" 22 times over

the course of thousands of words and every section of his memoir, from Hawaii – the site of visits and late evenings together – to Los Angeles to Chicago to Germany to Africa, from adolescence to college to community organizing. Davis is always one of the few (and first) names mentioned by Obama in each milemarker upon his historic path to Washington. When Davis is not physically there with Obama, Obama literally imagines him there. Obama felt a connection to "Frank" that he painfully concedes he was unable to find in anyone else.

Though Frank Marshall Davis's influence on Obama is acknowledged in *Dreams*, Obama never once disclosed the CPUSA member's full name. No doubt this was because Obama knew about Davis's extreme past, and preferred to want to disassociate himself from the extreme politics of an old CPUSA hack journalist. As Obama got closer to a run for the presidency, and released a 2005 audio version of *Dreams*, every single mention of "Frank" was magically purged. Not a single reference remained.

I believe that Davis is reflective, and helps explain, how and why America's current president is further to the left than any president of our generation. Davis sheds light on how our president developed into a man of the left, ultimately ranked the most left-leaning member of the Senate by *National Journal* in the final year before Obama ran for president.[84]

And yet, this radical influence on our president has been thoroughly ignored by the media. Even more interesting are the journalists who have written full-scale biographies of Obama or who have done intimate profiles of his Hawaii years and have had to confront the matter of Frank Marshall Davis. It is fascinating to see how they have avoided or dismissed Davis or, in some cases, avoided or dismissed those who have raised the specter of Davis. Consider just a few examples:

First came two profiles of Obama's Hawaii years

by the Associated Press, published at the height of the 2008 presidential campaign.[85] The fact that they would come during the campaign was itself a surefire predictor that they would be puff pieces ignoring the elephant in the Honolulu living room that was Frank Marshall Davis. Right on cue, the AP managed to scare up just one quotation from Davis amid all of his horribly pro-communist, anti-American writings. It was an isolated line showing Davis to be a grand constitutional freedom fighter. "I refuse to settle for anything less than all the rights which are due me under the constitution," said Davis stoically. According to the AP narrative, Davis was a champion of social justice, "his activism was aimed squarely at social injustice." Any suggestion that Davis harbored "allegedly anti-American views" was, insisted the AP, soundly rejected by "those who knew Davis and his work."

By the AP's telling, Davis, constitutional crusader, was a brave battler for "civil rights amid segregation," suffering the jackboot of segregation and racism. Ironically, this was a racism that Davis had laid at the feet of Harry Truman and the Democratic White House. Why? Because, again, Truman had the moral effrontery to dare to oppose Stalin and the communists. Predictably, however, there was not even one mention in the AP's story of any of this. The word "communism" was a total no-show by this premier media outlet.

This was journalistic malpractice. But, to be fair to the AP, it did nothing worse than any other major journalistic enterprise that ignored or downplayed Frank Marshall Davis. They were all united in their liberalism and liberal bias, and thus their duty to protect Barack Obama above all else.

Likewise performing its pro-Obama duties was the *Washington Post*, which, during the 2008 campaign, placed veteran reporter David Maraniss on a story about Obama's Hawaii experience. Maraniss chimed in with a major piece: a massive 10,000-word profile published in the August 22, 2008 edition of the *Post*. This was the time of the Democratic and Republican conventions. Thus, should one have expected any word of Frank Marshall Davis anywhere in the *Post*? Given the *Post*'s duty to liberal politics first and journalism second, the answer was a firm no. And those expectations were confirmed: Of the 10,000 words in the huge article, there was not one mention of Frank Marshall Davis.[86]

Notably, even Barack Obama himself could not do that, mentioning Davis up and down and throughout every section of his memoirs, even long after his Hawaii years. Obama was more honest than the *Washington Post*.

Of course, the *Post*'s Obama bias has always been blatant. And this was blatant.

The next day, August 23, *Newsweek*'s star reporter Jon Meacham published a piece on Obama's Hawaii years. Meacham did better than the *Post*. He at least mentioned Obama's mentor. But he did worse by defending Frank Marshall Davis and using the other approach of Davis's and Obama's defenders: attack the critics. And when he did, his reporting on Davis simply was not accurate.

Meacham claimed that Davis's innocent "political activism" – i.e., advocating not communism but "civil-rights and labor issues" – got him in trouble with Joe McCarthy and "HUAC." According to Meacham, Davis's "writings on civil-rights and labor issues" had "prompted a McCarthyite denunciation by the House Un-American Activities Committee."[87]

That was not true. Joe McCarthy never came anywhere near Frank Marshall Davis, nor did the House Committee on Un-American Activities. (McCarthy, as a senator, was never a member of the House Committee.) Rather, it was the Democrat-run Senate that summoned Davis to testify on his "pro-Sovietism" in December 1956 and that publicly and accurately referred to him as "an identified member of the Communist Party."

But again, why pick on Jon Meacham? He was simply doing what everyone in the mainstream media was doing: protecting Barack Obama. As he did, he was also covering for a terribly divisive and destructive American communist.

This was likewise true for David Remnick, the Pulitzer Prize winner and *Washington Post* and *New Yorker* journalist. Ironically, Remnick had been a reliable reporter on Soviet communism, and had written superb books on the subject, including his excellent 1994 work, *Lenin's Tomb*. Remnick was free to pursue excellence in that endeavor: exposing those truths about communism in the Cold War past had nothing to do with exposing truths about communism in Barack Obama's past. Unlike his piercing gaze into the Evil Empire, when Remnick looked into Obama's past and saw Frank Marshall Davis, he saw no evil. And so, as Remnick sought to write the definitive biographical work on Obama, titled, *The Bridge*, he would definitively downplay Frank Marshall Davis.[88]

In Remnick's hands, the old agitating CPUSA member had morphed into "one of the more interesting men in Honolulu," but not because of anything negative. Rather, Davis was the sympathetic grandson of a slave, a survivor of a "land of lynchings and frontier racism," a champion of "social justice," blessed with a "fantastically deep Barry White voice," and who had persevered to create a "distinguished career as a columnist and editor in the world of the black press." Here again, Davis was presented as nothing more than a marvelous civil-rights crusader fighting recalcitrant racists.

In service of the greater journalistic goal of advancing Barack Obama, Remnick took decades of personally keen insight into communists and their dealings and ignited it in flames. His past hard-earned experience as a seasoned reporter suddenly fell victim to self-imposed ignorance and naiveté, a refusal to want to see the truth. In the section of his book mentioning

Davis, the words "CPUSA," "Soviet Union," "Russia," "USSR," "communist," "Marxist," or any of the other words that dominated the life of Frank Marshall Davis for 50 years, vanished into the howling, desolate wilds of Siberia. Remnick resurrected just one of the words one time, and in service against the anti-communists who had been so rightly concerned with Davis's work on behalf of Stalin's state. This came in Remnick's discussion of how the insidious "right-wing blogosphere" was besmirching Obama's presidential bid by dragging in poor Davis as (in Remnick's words) "a card-carrying Communist, a pornographer, a pernicious influence. The attacks were loud and unrelenting."

Liberals reading Remnick's narrative would have concluded that such people were almost criminal in their irresponsibility and meanness. Where would they have conjured up such lunacy? After all, in Remnick's treatment, no such Frank Marshall Davis had ever existed. *Card-carrying Communist? Huh? What? Where? This is kooky, right-wing conspiracy talk at its worst!*

Finally, among the more disappointing treatments of the Davis matter was the work of the *Washington Post*'s Dana Milbank, who took the attack on Davis's critics to a new level. Milbank was dismissive of Davis because he was dismissive of the work of Cliff Kincaid and Herb Romerstein, who, at a May 2008 America's Survival press conference, divulged what they had found on Davis. What they found was stunning. Their findings made not only Davis look bad but, by extension, the young man that Davis influenced: Obama. It was that, no doubt, that bothered Milbank and thrust him into defensive mode: the reflexive posture of any journalist when conservatives criticize Obama or blow the whistle on his radical past associations. To liberals, this is an unacceptable injustice, utterly intolerable. They rally around their Obama like knights defending their castle.

Rather than consider Kincaid's and Romerstein's many irrefutable primary-source exhibits on Davis,

Milbank mocked and ridiculed both men, caricaturing their press conference as a conspiracy theorist's dream, a gathering of right-wing whackos – "a UFO convention."[89] They might as well have staged their carnival in Roswell, New Mexico, aside dummies of dead aliens. In a quite cruel gesture, Milbank referred to the widely respected Romerstein, who was America's leading authority on the Venona papers, as "a living relic from the House Committee on Un-American Activities." When Kincaid raised the fully legitimate point that Obama would have trouble getting a security clearance because of his remarkably troubling associations with the likes of Davis and Bill Ayers and others, Milbank merely laughed.[90]

But why laugh? To repeat: Frank Marshall Davis was actually placed on the federal government's Security Index. And this man was a significant influence on the young Obama. Would Milbank have scoffed if a Mitt Romney mentor from the far right had been placed on the government's Security Index?

No, he certainly would not. And neither would any journalist anywhere in the mainstream media.

What explains the double standard by Milbank, Remnick, Meacham, Maraniss, the AP, and all the others? We all know the obvious answer: Barack Obama. Because Frank Marshall Davis was an influence on Obama, liberal journalists have been forced to cover for Davis. It's that simple, and no mystery at all. Ironically, then, Davis, the old hardened CPUSA member, can – in death – continue to count on liberal/progressive journalists as dupes who will help cover his tracks. His work for Stalin's Soviet Union is once again protected by liberal/progressive journalists.

Some things truly do never change.

Chapter 8

The Preferred Enemy

Most of the journalists listed in this report were (in varying degrees) dupes; that is, genuine liberal/progressive Americans who unwittingly did the bidding of communists and international communism. There was no malice intended or evil ruthlessly pursued. They did not deliberately set out to consciously serve as agents advancing communist objectives. There were some journalists, however, who were actual communists or agents of communists, who worked quite wittingly for the accomplishment of Marxist-Leninist objectives. Often still to this today, it is hard to know which was which. We may yet come upon a smoking gun somewhere in Soviet archives revealing at long last that this or that suspected duped journalist was something much more sinister. If and when we do, few reading this report will be surprised. The liberal media, however, will be surprised, and will ignore it.

But whether the journalist (innocent or not) was a Walter Duranty stumping for Stalin's five-year plans, or Herb Matthews rescuing Fidel and Che, or Edgar Snow crafting an advertisement for Mao Tse-tung, or the *New York Times* doing what it usually does, the tragic result is frequently the same: history is moved in favor of America's adversaries. And international communism was no minor adversary; it was responsible for the deaths of at least 100 million people in the last century, and likely as high as 140 million.[91] For a sense of perspective, that is double the combined death tolls of

World War I and II. It dwarfs Hitler's Holocaust. Here is the saddest part of all: its destruction is far from over. Communism still jails and represses in China. It continues to squash private property and basic civil liberties in Cuba. It generates boat people in Vietnam. Its policy prescriptions aren't finished making people poor in Zimbabwe or starving them in North Korea.

Even here in America, it somehow continues to have its advocates, not to mention a resurgence in some circles. Modern practitioners often call themselves something else, doing what communists did in the 1930s and 1940s and 1950s – sometimes describing themselves as good-hearted "progressives" pursuing "equality" and "social justice," other times as earth-friendly environmentalists wanting to restrain the excesses of capitalism or "Wall Street," and other times choosing some other label or cover. Remarkably, certain of these tacks have been employed by '60s communist radicals like Bill Ayers and Bernardine Dohrn and even the founders and members of the modern group Progressives for Obama: Tom Hayden, Mark Rudd, Carl Davidson, Jane Fonda, Daniel Ellsberg, Todd Gitlin, and many more.[92] Many were literal communists or sympathizers in the 1960s. Today, they are self-described "progressives" battling for Barack Obama on websites, on Facebook, from Twitter feeds, and from university lecterns.

Here is the biggest irony of all: As they do their work to advance the boundaries of the extreme left, those most often condemned are the *anti*-communists who blow the whistle and cry foul, daring to expose them for who they were and what they are up to today. Who leads the choir of condemnation? Who most resoundingly condemns the anti-communist whistleblowers, doing so with credibility that the communist left does not have? The same group that communists have always been able to depend upon to stop their accusers: duped liberal/progressive journalists.

For these liberal/progressive journalists, what's the

news that's fit to print? What is the typical storyline? It is often one that frames the anti-communists as the paranoid bad guys. Still today, well into the 21st century, every new anti-communist or anti-communist revelation prompts liberal journalists to wring their hands in fear not of yet another communist death or repression but yet another supposed surge of "McCarthyism." Indeed, many on the left still view anti-communism generally as not far removed from McCarthyism, and as more loathsome and dangerous than pro-communism. As it was put it in a major Cold War feature for *New York Times Magazine*, "while Communists may have been wrong in their views, McCarthyism was the greater evil."[93] Or still, as another recent journalist put it in the *New York Review of Books*, the real danger was not American communism, which "never controlled a major city or region, or even elected a single member to a national legislature," but American anti-communism and its "heresy hunters," which "destroyed thousands of careers; witch-hunted dissidents in Hollywood, universities, and government departments; and was a force that politicians like Joseph McCarthy and Richard Nixon rode to national prominence."[94]

This, of course, is preposterous. American communists never needed to control a city or region or the movie industry or an entire university or government department. Their *influence* – whether on policy or events in China, Cuba, Poland, Korea, Vietnam, etc. – was often just enough.

But for America's liberals/progressives, the anti-communist is the influence that must be most feared. That's the left's thinking in a nutshell. As James Burnham, the great convert to anti-communism, famously remarked: for the left, "the preferred enemy is always to the right"–never to the left.[95]

And so, when a specter like Frank Marshall Davis is identified from the not-too-distant past as a formative figure in the development of the current president of the United States and leader of the free world – so identified by the likes of myself, Cliff Kincaid, the late Herb Romerstein, and others – it is we identifiers whose work is besmirched and whose reputations are attacked. It is, yet again, the anti-communists who are portrayed as the extremists, as the bad guys – the preferred enemy to the right. In the meantime, the likes of Davis, like the CPUSA members and outright Stalinists before him, get a pass by the very same liberal media that has held its (biased) grip on America for at least a century. Those laughing loudest are those from the communist left that still get protected. Some of them howl from their graves.

In the end, who or what is best served, whether intentionally or not? The answer is America's adversaries. They are aided and abetted in their misbegotten efforts to alter the course of history in their favor. Duped liberal/progressive journalists continue to be their handmaiden.

Appendix

A Popular Russian
Oleg Danilovich Kalugin

ONE of the results of the Soviet-American student exchange is that the student council of Columbia University's School of Journalism now includes a Soviet citizen, elected by his classmates. He is 24-year-old Oleg Danilovich Kalugin of Leningrad. "Brilliant" and "a real personality kid" are typical of the terms Columbia professors and students apply to Mr. Kalugin. With an engaging smile and fluent English, this blond, slim, jaunty young man has won many friends since he arrived on the Columbia campus six months ago.

Part of the reason for his popularity at the School of Journalism has been his willingness to enter into the spirit of the work there. Typical was the time several weeks ago when he and a student-photographer went to the Metropolitan Opera House and took pictures of the Bolshoi Ballet's ballerinas during their rehearsals, sometimes in ungraceful poses. Mr. Kalugin was not daunted by the fact that he and his colleague were thrown out of the Metropolitan when their unauthorized presence was discovered.

Many Tastes in Common

Another reason for Mr. Kalugin's popularity is that he has many tastes in common with his fellow students. He is a jazz fan, favoring the music of Glenn Miller and Harry James. He does not like rock 'n' roll.

"The United States is just what I expected it to be," Mr. Kalugin says, stoutly denying that the Soviet press distorts American realities. A member of the Young Communist League, he expects to join the Communist party. Since arriving here he has had many discussions on political matters with Americans who disagree with his Communist views. He has also expressed his views before an audience of school children in Darien, Conn.

Mr. Kalugin spends much of his spare time at the movies, a habit he has brought from home where he usually saw more than 100 pictures yearly. So far he has seen about seventy films here, all of which he has carefully listed and rated. "The Old Man and the Sea," is his favorite American film so far.

He thinks Soviet journalists can learn some things from American practice, particularly the speed of sending the main news of a story of the abbreviated form used in cables for transmitting messages. He has enjoyed the School of Journalism, but has some criticisms too, saying: "I think the courses are too practical. There should be more courses giving background information."

Majored in U. S. Literature

Mr. Kalugin specialized in American literature at the University of Leningrad. For his visit here he was selected by his professors and Soviet educational authorities on the basis of his knowledge of English and general ability.

Born in Leningrad Sept. 6, 1934, Mr. Kalugin was evacuated from that city soon after the German attack in 1941 and spent most of the war years with his mother in the Siberian city of Omsk. His father, a clerk in Leningrad's city government, stayed in the city throughout the siege. Mr. Kalugin is an only child.

Like many a young American, he began dating his wife, Ludmilla, early, when he was 16, and married her four years later. His wife who has remained in Leningrad, is a mathematics teacher. Mr. Kalugin, noting the wide differences between his own and his wife's interests, says, "I was afraid it might be boring, but so far it hasn't been." The Kalugins have a 3-year-old daughter, Svetlana.

"Real personality kid"

Figure 1. Oleg Kalugin in the *New York Times*

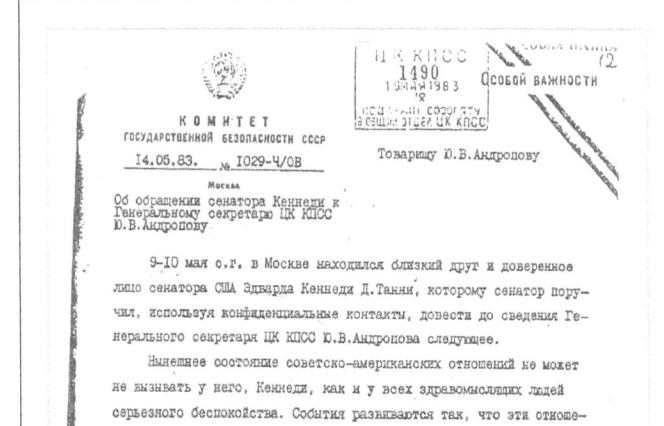

Figure 2. Senator Kennedy's request to Andropov, 1983 [translation follows]

рые скрытые тенденции, которые способны привести к новому серьезному осложнению экономического положения в США. Произойти это может в самый разгар президентской избирательной кампании 1984 года, что было бы на руку демократической партии. Однако твердой уверенности в таком развитии событий пока нет.

Пожалуй, единственным потенциально опасным для Рейгана вопросом становятся проблемы войны и мира и советско-американских отношений. Этот вопрос, как считает сенатор, несомненно будет важным фактором в избирательной кампании. В Соединенных Штатах ширится движение за замораживание ядерных арсеналов обеих стран, предпринимаются, в том числе и им, Кеннеди, меры к его дальнейшей активизации. В политических, деловых кругах страны, в конгрессе возрастает сопротивление непомерному наращиванию военных расходов.

И все же, по мнению Кеннеди, оппозиция Рейгану еще слаба. Выступления противников президента разрозненны и недостаточно эффективны, а Рейган обладает возможностями вести успешную контрпропаганду. С целью нейтрализовать критику в свой адрес по поводу неконструктивности линии США на переговорах с СССР, Рейган готов и дальше выдвигать внешне броские, но по существу лишь пропагандистские инициативы. В то же время инициативы и выступления советских руководителей в области ограничения вооружений часто искажаются, замалчиваются или просто огульно отвергаются под любым надуманным предлогом. Самим американцам в сути этих сложных вопросов разобраться трудно, да и аргументы советской стороны до них иногда не доходят. Хотя изложение выступлений руководителей СССР и помещают в прессе, нельзя не учитывать, что большинство американцев не читает серьезных газет и журналов.

Кеннеди полагает, что в данной обстановке в интересах дела мира было бы полезным и своевременным предпринять некоторые дополнительные шаги по противодействию милитаристской политике Рейгана и его кампании психологического давления на американское население. В этой связи он хотел бы обратиться к Генеральному секретарю ЦК КПСС Ю.В.Андропову со следующими предложениями:

1. Кеннеди просил бы Ю.В.Андропова рассмотреть вопрос о возможности принять его в Москве для личной беседы в июле с.г. Главную цель встречи сенатор видит в том, чтобы вооружиться разъяснениями советского руководителя по проблемам ограничения ядерных вооружений и использовать их в последующем для более убедительных выступлений в США. В этой связи он хотел бы проинформировать, что им также запланирована поездка в Западную Европу, где, в частности, предусмотрены встречи с премьер-министром Англии Тэтчер и президентом Франции Миттераном, с которыми он намерен обменяться мнениями по тем же проблемам.

Если просьба о приеме его Ю.В.Андроповым будет сочтена в принципе приемлемой, Кеннеди направит в Москву своего представителя для решения вопросов, связанных с организацией поездки.

Кеннеди считает, что позитивное влияние беседы с Ю.В.Андроповым на общественность и политические круги США может оказаться еще большим, если он пригласит с собой кого-либо из видных сенаторов-республиканцев, например Марка Хэтфилда. (Хэтфилд совместно с Кеннеди в марте 1982 года выдвинул проект резолюции о замораживании ядерных арсеналов США и СССР и опубликовал книгу на ту же тему).

2. Кеннеди полагает, что с точки зрения воздействия на умонастроения американцев было бы желательным организовать в августе-сентябре с.г. интервью Ю.В.Андропова для телевидения США. Такое непосредственное обращение Генерального секретаря ЦК КПСС к американскому народу несомненно вызовет огромное внимание и интерес в стране. Сенатор убежден, что оно получит максимальный резонанс, ибо телевидение в США - наиболее эффективное средство массовой

информации.

Если это предложение будет сочтено заслуживающим внимания, то Кеннеди и его друзья предпримут соответствующие шаги, чтобы кто-либо из представителей крупнейших телекомпаний США обратился к Ю.В.Андропову с просьбой принять его в Москве и дать интервью. В Москву, в частности, могли бы прибыть председатель совета директоров телевизионной компании "Эй-Би-Си" Элтон Рул, обозреватели Уолтер Кронкайт или Барбара Уолтерс. Важно, подчеркнул сенатор, что инициатива при этом будет исходить от американской стороны.

Затем в тех же целях можно организовать серию интервью для телевидения США ряда советских деятелей, в том числе военных. Они также получили бы возможность непосредственно обратиться к американскому народу с разъяснением мирных инициатив СССР, со своей аргументацией относительно того, каков же истинный баланс сил СССР и США в военной области. А этот вопрос особенно грубо искажается администрацией Рейгана.

Кеннеди просил передать, что это обращение к Генеральному секретарю ЦК КПСС объясняется его стремлением внести посильный вклад в дело устранения угрозы ядерной войны, улучшения советско-американских отношений, которые он считает определяющими для сохранения мира. На него, Кеннеди, производит большое впечатление активная деятельность Ю.В.Андропова вместе с другими советскими руководителями, направленная на оздоровление международной обстановки, улучшение взаимопонимания между народами.

Сенатор подчеркнул, что будет с нетерпением ждать ответа на свое обращение, который можно довести до него через Тапни.

Изложив обращение Кеннеди к Генеральному секретарю ЦК КПСС Ю.В.Андропову, Тапни рассказал, что сенатор Кеннеди в последнее время активизирует выступления в пользу устранения угрозы войны. Формальный отказ от участия в избирательной кампании 1984 года

...пособствовал тому, что высказывания сенатора воспринимаются в
США не предвзято, так как они не связаны с предвыборными соображ-
ениями. Танни отметил, что сенатор нацелен на то, чтобы добиться
избрания на пост президента США в 1988 году. К тому времени ему
исполнится 56 лет, будут устранены проблемы личного плана, которые ослабляли его положение (Кеннеди без излишней шумихи закончил
бракоразводный процесс и вскоре планирует повторно вступить в
брак). Вместе с тем Кеннеди не исключает, что в избирательной кампании 1984 года может возникнуть ситуация, когда демократическая
партия официально обратится к нему с просьбой возглавить ее в
борьбе против республиканцев и добиваться избрания президентом.
Это объясняется тем, что ни один из нынешних претендентов от демо-
кратов не имеет реальных шансов на победу над Рейганом.

Просим указаний.

Председатель Комитета *[signature]* В.Чебриков

Special Importance

Committee on State Security of the USSR
14.05.1983 No. 1029 Ch/OV
Moscow

Regarding Senator Kennedy's request to the General Secretary of the Communist Party Y. V. Andropov

Comrade Y. V. Andropov

On 9-10 May of this year, Senator Edward Kennedy's close friend and trusted confidant J. Tunney was in Moscow. The senator charged Tunney to convey the following message, through confidential contacts, to the General Secretary of the Central Committee of the Communist Party of the Soviet Union, Y. Andropov:

Senator Kennedy, like other rational people, is very troubled by the current state of Soviet-American relations. Events are developing such that this relationship coupled with the general state of global affairs will make the situation even more dangerous. The main reason for this is Reagan's belligerence, and his firm commitment to deploy new American middle range nuclear weapons within Western Europe.

According to Kennedy, the current threat is due to the President's refusal to engage any modification to his politics. He feels that his domestic standing has been strengthened because of the well publicized improvement of the economy: inflation has been greatly reduced, production levels are increasing as is overall business activity. For these reasons, interest rates will continue to decline. The White House has portrayed this in the media as the "success of Reaganomics."

Naturally, not everything in the province of economics has gone according to Reagan's plan. A few well known economists and members of financial circles, particularly from the north-eastern states, foresee certain hidden tendencies that may bring about a new economic crisis in the USA. This could bring about the fall of the presidential campaign of 1984, which would benefit the Democratic party. Nevertheless, there are no secure assurances this will indeed develop.

The only real potential threats to Reagan are problems of war and peace and Soviet-American relations. These issues, according to the senator, will without a doubt become the most important of the election campaign. The movement advocating a freeze on nuclear arsenals of both countries continues to gain strength in the United States. The movement is also willing to accept preparations, particularly from Kennedy, for its continued growth. In political and influential circles of the country, including within Congress, the resistance to growing military expenditures is gaining strength.

However, according to Kennedy, the opposition to Reagan is still very weak. Reagan's adversaries are divided and the presentations they make are not fully effective. Meanwhile, Reagan has the capabilities to effectively counter any propaganda. In order to neutralize criticism that the talks between the USA and USSR are non-constructive, Reagan will be grandiose, but subjectively propagandistic. At the same time, Soviet officials who speak about disarmament will be quoted out of context, silenced or groundlessly and whimsically discounted. Although arguments and statements by officials of the USSR do appear in the press, it is important to note the majority of Americans do not read serious newspapers or periodicals.

Kennedy believes that, given the current state of affairs, and in the interest of peace, it would be prudent and timely to undertake the following steps to counter the militaristic politics of Reagan and his campaign to psychologically burden the American people. In this regard, he offers the following proposals to the General Secretary of the Central Committee of the Communist Party of the Soviet Union Y. V. Andropov:

1. Kennedy asks Y. V. Andropov to consider inviting the senator to Moscow for a personal meeting in July of this year. The main purpose of the meeting, according to the senator, would be to arm Soviet officials with explanations regarding problems of nuclear disarmament so they may be better prepared and more convincing during appearances in the USA. He would also like to inform you that he has planned a trip through Western Europe, where he anticipates meeting England's Prime Minister Margaret Thatcher and French President Mitterand in which he will exchange similar ideas regarding the same issues.

If his proposals would be accepted in principle, Kennedy would send his representative to Moscow to resolve questions regarding organizing such a visit.

Kennedy thinks the benefit of a meeting with Y. V. Andropov will be enhanced if he could also invite one of the well known Republican senators, for example, Mark Hatfield. Such a meeting will have a strong impact on Americans and political circles in the USA. (In March of 1982, Hatfield and Kennedy proposed a project resolution to freeze the nuclear arsenals of the USA and the USSR and published a book on this theme as well).

2. Kennedy believes that in order to influence Americans it would be important to organize in August-September of this year, televised interviews with Y. V. Andropov in the USA. A direct appeal by the General Secretary of the Central Committee of the Communist Party of the Soviet Union to the American people will, without a doubt, attract a great deal of attention and interest in the country. The senator is convinced this would receive the maximum resonance in so far as television is the most effective method of mass media and information.

If the proposal is recognized as worthy, then Kennedy and his friends will bring about suitable steps to have representatives of the largest television companies in the USA contact Y. V. Andropov for an invitation to Moscow for the interview. Specifically, the president of the board of directors of ABC, Elton Raul and television columnists Walter Conkrite or Barbara Walters could visit Moscow. The senator underlined the importance that this initiative should be seen as coming from the American side.

Furthermore, with the same purpose in mind, a series of televised interviews in the USA with lower level Soviet officials, particularly from the military would be organized. They would also have an opportunity to appeal directly to the American people about the peaceful intentions of the USSR, with their own arguments about maintaining a true balance of power between the USSR and the USA in military terms. This issue is quickly being distorted by Reagan's administration.

Kennedy asked to convey, that this appeal to the General Secretary of the Central Committee of the Communist Party of the Soviet Union is his effort to contribute a strong proposal that would root out the threat of nuclear war, and to improve Soviet-American relations, so that they define the safety for the world. Kennedy is very impressed with the activities of Y. V. Andropov and other Soviet leaders, who expressed their commitment to heal international affairs, and improve mutual understandings between peoples.

The senator underscored that he eagerly awaits a reply to his appeal, the answer to which may be delivered through Tunney.

Having conveyed Kennedy's appeal to the General Secretary of the Central Committee of the Communist Party of the Soviet Union, Tunney also explained that Senator Kennedy has in the last few years actively made appearances to reduce the threat of war. Because he formally refused to partake in the election campaign of 1984, his speeches would be taken without prejudice as they are not tied to any campaign promises. Tunney remarked that the senator wants to run for president in 1988. At that time, he will be 56 and his personal problems, which could hinder his standing, will be resolved (Kennedy has just completed a divorce and plans to re-marry in the near future). Taken together, Kennedy does not discount that during the 1984 campaign, the Democratic party may officially turn to him to lead the fight against the Republicans and elect their candidate president. This would explain why he is convinced that none of the candidates today have a real chance at defeating Reagan.

We await instructions.

President of the committee   V. Chebrikov

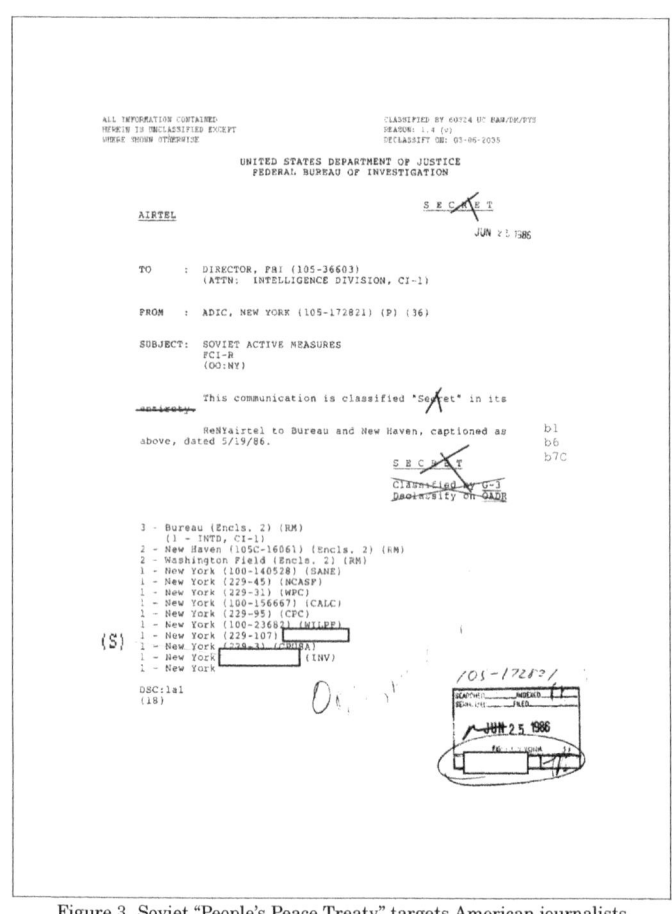

Figure 3. Soviet "People's Peace Treaty" targets American journalists

CAMPAIGN FOR A PEOPLE'S PEACE TREATY
162 Madison Avenue, New York, NY 10016

The Campaign Committee met at 1140 Broadway Sunday, May 18th. 15 persons were present.

The Committee received and considered three alternative redraftings of the Treaty. A committee of three will produce a new draft by the end of the week which Alan Thomson will take to the Soviet Peace Committee in Moscow next week.

It was AGREED that the Campaign will seek both individual signatures and organizational endorsements to the treaty.

Several alternative locations for an office were considered. A decision will be made at the next meeting. Members are asked to suggest possible staff people.

Roger Powers agreed to report on the Treaty to the meeting of peace organizations in Philadelphia May 21st.

The new Treaty draft will be available with a covering letter to be sent to potential endorsers.

Possible members of the US delegation to sign the Treaty were discussed:

1. Military person - from Center for Defense Information
2. Scientist -
3. Clergy -
4. Medical
5. Education
6. Youth - Winner of PEP Contest
7. Veteran - someone from Veterans for Peace
8. Labor -
9. Artist
10. Homemaker
11. Athlete
12. Elected Official -
13. Industry - Armand
14. Senior -
15. Media - Walter Cronkite, Harrison Salisbury, David Brinkley, Bill Moyers

The final group should have thirteen members. Committee members have agreed to seek out people on the above list after the final treaty text is available.

The next meeting will be held on Sunday, June 15th at 1140 Broadway, Rm. 401 at 2:00 p.m.

SECRET

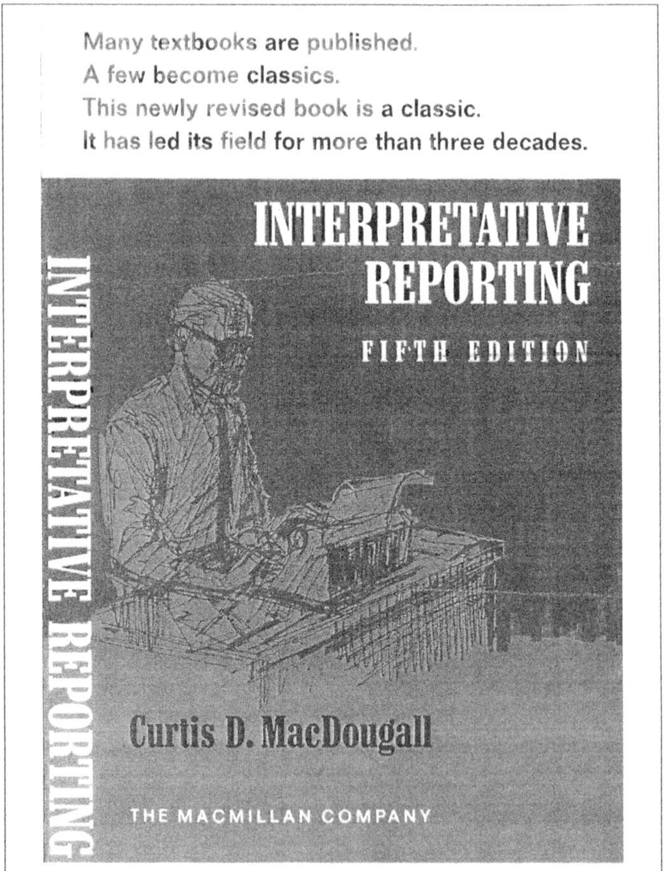
Many textbooks are published.
A few become classics.
This newly revised book is a classic.
It has led its field for more than three decades.
INTERPRETATIVE REPORTING
FIFTH EDITION
INTERPRETATIVE REPORTING
Curtis D. MacDougall
THE MACMILLAN COMPANY

Figure 4. Interpretative Reporting

Figure 5. Obama mentor Frank Marshall Davis' *Star* promoting Curtis MacDougall for Illinois Senate

MacDougall back in Senate race

Curtis D. MacDougall, Northwestern University journalism professor, will be the Progressive Party's candidate for U. S. Senator in November.

MacDougall, who withdrew from the slate last week because NU officials threatened to fire him, reconsidered his decision and accepted the nomination.

It was understood that widespread protests against the university's undemocratic attitude had convinced MacDougall that the people want him for their candidate.

* * *

THE PROGRESSIVES were "delighted" by his decision to run for the Senate seat. William Miller, state director of the new party, said:

"It is the gain of the people of Illinois that they will have an opportunity in November of 1948 to elect to the U. S. Senate a man of great principle, deep understanding, and real courage."

In his letter of acceptance, MacDougall declared:

"The circumstances which caused me to decline this nomination have not changed. I have simply concluded personal considerations, however urgent, must take second place in this period of real and great crisis.

"This conviction is not new with me. I have long believed that nobody justifiably can put personal security or comfort ahead of his obligation to democracy. That I can be among those able to apply this principle to his own life is a source of great pride."

List names of Progressive nominees for state offices

The state ticket of the Progressive Party was completed this week. The most recent additions to the slate are listed below. Next week the entire state and county ticks will be listed.

ATTORNEY GENERAL: Don Hesson attorney, economist, and world traveler.

TREASURER: Fred J. Nelson, business man of Belleville.

AUDITOR OF PUBLIC ACCOUNTS: Bernard J. McDonough, president of Local 1119, United Electrical, Radio & Machine Workers of America (CIO), and president of the People's Publishing Assn., membership organization which controls The Chicago Star.

SECRETARY OF STATE: Rebecca Styles Taylor, columnist for the Chicago Defender, local Negro newspaper.

TRUSTEES OF THE UNIVERSITY OF ILLINOIS: Mrs. Anita McCormick Blaine, daughter of the late Cyrus Hall McCormick, inventor of the reaping machine; the Rev. Wilfrid Wakefield, pastor of the First Congregational Church of Brookfield; and R. V. Cassill, professor of English at Monticello College.

9-week PP drive arrived at 125,000 signatures

With the July 23 deadline only nine weeks off, the Progressive Party this week prepared to swing into a drive for petitions to put Henry Wallace and Glen Taylor on the ballot in Illinois in November.

The opening of the campaign for signatures on petitions had been set originally for last Sunday, but difficulties in getting the petition forms printed delayed the drive.

Zal Garfield, county director, said that the Progressives had raised their goal from 100,000 to 125,000 signatures in order to provide a safe margin over the required number.

* * *

SOME 100,000 of the signatures will be sought in Cook County, with the remainder coming from 65 other counties including all of the 13 downstate Congressional districts.

The drive was expected to begin with a meeting of the county central committee at the Midland Hotel Friday night.

There w a r d committeemen were to receive their share of the petitions, which will be distributed to ward clubs during the next week or two.

Meanwhile, pro-Wallace students at downstate colleges are being asked to pledge their efforts during the petition drive after classes end for the summer.

Council group aiding Edison franchise steal

The Commonwealth Edison Co. of the 100 cities than they are

Figure 6. The *Star* stumps for MacDougall

Dewey, Truman face test in South, says MacDougall

AFRO, JULY 17, 1948

Are political party platform planks on civil rights sincere promises or "campaign oratory"?

That's a question that will be answered when Gov. Thomas E. Dewey and President Harry S. Truman, the Republican and Democratic Presidential nominees, tour the South, according to Curtis D. MacDougall, Progressive candidate for U. S. Senator.

"The honesty of the GOP and the Democratic platforms will be demonstrated when their candidates speak before segregated or non-segregated audiences in the South," the Northwestern University journalism professor told a rally at Freeport.

* * *

WALLACE and Taylor are the only candidates whose stand on racial equality cannot be questioned, MacDougall contended. He pointed out that Wallace always has refused to speak before segregated audiences in the South. And Sen. Glen Taylor recently was arrested at Birmingham, Ala., for defying jim crow laws.

MacDougall slammed into the Republican 80th Congress — and the Democrat-controlled 79th Congress which it followed — for failing to act on anti-lynch laws, anti-poll tax bills, fair employment proposals, and measures to outlaw attempts to incite racial hatred.

A FOUNDER of the Natl. Council of Negro Women and a leader of the Natl. Federation of Colored Women, Mrs. Rebecca Stiles Taylor is also one of the most active Wallace workers in Illinois. Candidate for secretary of state, she also is co-chairman of Chicago Women for Wallace.

Times-men for PP

NEW YORK—The composing room of the august New York Times, whose publisher has hired varitypers in preparation for a lock-out of AFL Typographical Union members, has already turned in 150 signed pledge cards for Henry Wallace.

challenged

Figure 7. Frank Marshall Davis' *Star* continues to promote Curtis MacDougall

Sen. Taylor to speak at State Fair PP Day

Sen. Glen H. Taylor of Idaho, Progressive Party candidate for Vice President, will deliver an address during Progressive Party Day activities at the Illinois State Fair at Springfield this Saturday, Aug. 14.

Henry Wallace's running mate probably will fly here from New York to speak during the two and a half hour observances that will mark the second day of the fair.

No admission will be charged on Saturday.

* * *

GRANT OAKES, president of the United Farm Equipment & Metal Workers of America (CIO), will head the list of Illinois Progressive candidates who will speak.

As a candidate for governor, Oakes is expected to attack the Democratic and Republican failure to take action to solve crucial problems confronting the people of this state.

Other candidates who will speak include Curtis D. MacDougall, nominee for U. S. Senator; Mrs. Rebecca Stiles Taylor, Chicago Defender columnist and candidate for Illinois secretary of state; and Harry Diehl, Gibson City farmer-lawyer and nominee for lieutenant-governor. Studs Terkel, Chicago radio commentator, will be master of ceremonies.

* * *

OTHER FEATURES of the day will include group singing led by Bernie Asbel and Win Stracke, folksingers, with a local band, plus skits presented by Arts for Wallace.

The Progressive Party activities will take place in front of the race track grandstand from 11 a.m. to 1:30 p.m.

* * *

COOK COUNTY Progressives

Figure 8. More stumping for MacDougall and his fellow "progressives" by Obama's mentor's newspaper

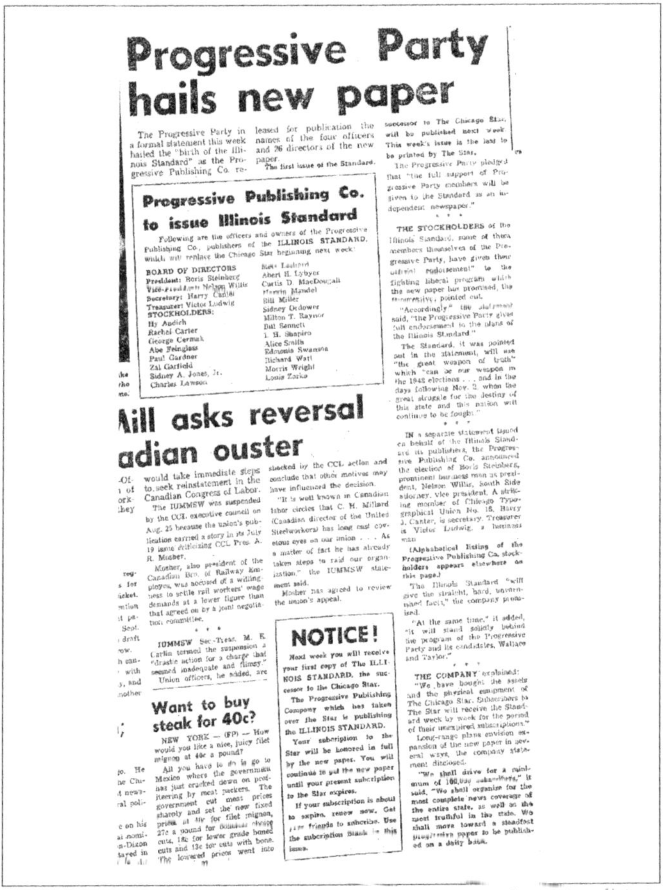

Progressive Party hails new paper

The Progressive Party in a formal statement this week hailed the "birth of the Illinois Standard" as the Progressive Publishing Co. released for publication the names of the four officers and 26 directors of the new paper.

The first issue of the Standard, successor to The Chicago Star, will be published next week. This week's issue is the last to be printed by The Star.

The Progressive Party pledged that "the full support of Progressive Party members will be given to the Standard as an independent newspaper."

* * *

THE STOCKHOLDERS of the Illinois Standard, some of them members themselves of the Progressive Party, have given their official endorsement" to the fighting liberal program which the new paper has promised, the progressives pointed out.

"Accordingly," the statement said, "the Progressive Party gives full endorsement to the plans of the Illinois Standard."

The Standard, it was pointed out in the statement, will use "the great weapon of truth" which "can be our weapon in the 1948 elections . . . and in the days following Nov. 2, when the great struggle for the destiny of this state and this nation will continue to be fought."

* * *

IN a separate statement issued on behalf of the Illinois Standard its publishers, the Progressive Publishing Co. announced the election of Boris Steinberg, prominent business man as president, Nelson Willis, South Side attorney, vice president. A striking member of Chicago Typographical Union No. 16, Harry J. Canter, is secretary. Treasurer is Victor Ludwig, a business man.

(Alphabetical listing of the Progressive Publishing Co. stockholders appears elsewhere on this page.)

The Illinois Standard "will give the straight, hard, unvarnished facts," the company promised.

"At the same time," it added, "it will stand solidly behind the program of the Progressive Party and its candidates, Wallace and Taylor."

* * *

THE COMPANY explained: "We have bought the assets and the physical equipment of The Chicago Star. Subscribers to The Star will receive the Standard week by week for the period of their unexpired subscriptions."

Long-range plans envision expansion of the new paper in several ways, the company statement disclosed.

"We shall drive for a minimum of 100,000 subscribers," it said. "We shall organize for the most complete news coverage of the entire state, as well as the most truthful in the state. We shall move toward a steadfast progressive paper to be published on a daily basis.

Progressive Publishing Co. to issue Illinois Standard

Following are the officers and owners of the Progressive Publishing Co., publishers of the ILLINOIS STANDARD, which will replace the Chicago Star beginning next week:

BOARD OF DIRECTORS
President: Boris Steinberg
Vice-President: Nelson Willis
Secretary: Harry Canter
Treasurer: Victor Ludwig
STOCKHOLDERS:
Hy Audich
Rachel Carter
George Cermak
Abe Feinglass
Paul Gardner
Zal Garfield
Sidney A. Jones, Jr.
Charles Lawson
Ross Lashord
Abert H. Lybyer
Curtis D. MacDougall
Marvin Mandel
Bill Miller
Sidney Ordower
Milton T. Raynor
Bill Sennett
I. H. Shapiro
Alice Smith
Edmonia Swanson
Richard Watt
Morris Wright
Louis Zorko

Aill asks reversal adian ouster

would take immediate steps to seek reinstatement in the Canadian Congress of Labor.

The IUMMSW was suspended by the CCL executive council on Aug. 25 because the union's publication carried a story in its July 19 issue criticizing CCL Pres. A. R. Mosher.

Mosher, also president of the Canadian Bro. of Railway Employes, was accused of a willingness to settle rail workers' wage demands at a lower figure than that agreed on by a joint negotiation committee.

* * *

IUMMSW Sec.-Treas. M. E. Carlin termed the suspension a "drastic action for a charge that seemed inadequate and flimsy."

Union officers, he added, are shocked by the CCL action and conclude that other motives may have influenced the decision.

"It is well known in Canadian labor circles that C. H. Millard (Canadian director of the United Steelworkers) has long cast covetous eyes on our union . . . As a matter of fact he has already taken steps to raid our organization," the IUMMSW statement said.

Mosher has agreed to review the union's appeal.

Want to buy steak for 40c?

NEW YORK — (FP) — How would you like a nice, juicy filet mignon at 40c a pound?

All you have to do is go to Mexico where the government has just cracked down on profiteering by meat packers. The government cut meat prices sharply and set the new fixed price at 40c for filet mignon, 27c a pound for ordinary choice cuts, 18c for lower grade boned cuts and 13c for cuts with bone. The lowered prices went into

NOTICE!

Next week you will receive your first copy of The ILLINOIS STANDARD, the successor to the Chicago Star.

The Progressive Publishing Company which has taken over the Star is publishing the ILLINOIS STANDARD.

Your subscription to the Star will be honored in full by the new paper. You will continue to get the new paper until your present subscription to the Star expires.

If your subscription is about to expire, renew now. Get your friends to subscribe. Use the subscription blank in this issue.

Figure 9. Final issue of Frank Marshall Davis' *Star* – note the curious list of "progressive" purchasers

Figure 10. A notable communist front's fascinating list of officers/members, including a congressman or two, and a presidential mentor (please pardon the poor image quality)

Endnotes

[1] I say "not usually intentional" because there have been communists at the *New York Times*. In the 1930s, for instance, there was a unit of communist reporters at the *Times*, which fancied itself as an actual "branch" of the *Times*. These reporters splintered off and created a rival spin-off publication, a monthly called *The New Times*. It billed itself as "Published Every Month by the Communist Party Branch of the *New York Times*." Congress even went so far as to investigate this unit or "cell."

[2] "A Popular Russian: Oleg Danilovich Kalugin," *The New York Times*, May 11, 1959, p. 7.

[3] For numerous examples, see "Columbia University" in the index of my book, *Dupes: How America's Adversaries Have Manipulated Progressives for a Century* (Wilmington, Delaware: ISI Books, 2010).

[4] Oleg Kalugin, *The First Directorate: My 32 Years in Intelligence and Espionage Against the West* (NY: St. Martin's Press, 1994), p. 1.

[5] The *Times* article did not list a byline.

[6] The collection of essays was published in 1929 by The New Republic, Inc., as well as in subsequent Dewey writings and a later (1964) volume edited by William W. Brickman, produced and published by the Teachers College at Columbia University. William W. Brickman, ed., *John Dewey's Impressions of Soviet Russia and the Revolutionary World, Mexico-China-Turkey 1929* (NY: Bureau of Publications, Teachers College, Columbia University, 1964).

[7] Brickman, ed., *John Dewey's Impressions*, pp. 54-5.

[8] Ibid.

[9] Ibid, pp. 110-1.

[10] Interestingly, the remainder of the quote (usually not noted) reads: "That is my belief. But I don't want to live there." Among others, see the discussion in Paul Hollander, *Political Pilgrims* (NY: Harper & Row, 1983), p. 64.

[11] "Guide to Subversive Organizations and Publications" (and Appendices), revised and published December 1, 1961, to supersede Guide published on January 2, 1957 (including Index), prepared and released by the Committee on Un-American Activities, U.S. House

of Representatives, Washington, DC, 87th Congress, 2nd Session, House Document No, 398, p. 77.

[12] William Z. Foster, *Toward Soviet America* (NY: International Publishers, 1932), pp. 272-3.

[13] To view the photo and other details, see: Kengor, *Dupes*, pp. 71-2.

[14] The definitive work on this subject is S. J. Taylor, *Stalin's Apologist: Walter Duranty: The New York Times's Man in Moscow* (NY: Oxford University Press, 1990).

[15] Eugene Lyons, *The Red Decade: Stalinist Penetration of America* (Indianapolis: Bobbs-Merrill, 1941), p. 123.

[16] Malcolm Muggeridge, *The Sun Never Sets* (NY: Random House, 1940), p. 79.

[17] Malcolm Muggeridge, *Chronicles of Wasted Time, Chronicle 1: The Green Stick* (NY: Quill, 1982), pp. 255-6.

[18] Ibid.

[19] Ibid.

[20] See http://www.ifstone.org/biography-refuted.php, the I. F. Stone tribute website. The *Los Angeles Times* dubbed Stone the "conscience of investigative journalism," and CNN's Larry King called him a "hero." An Oliphant cartoon showed Stone outside the Pearly Gates, with Saint Peter telephoning God, "Yes, THAT I. F. Stone, Sir. He says he doesn't want to come in – he'd rather hang around out here, and keep things honest."

[21] In an article excerpted from the book and published in the April 2009 online version of *Commentary* magazine, titled, "Special Preview: I.F. Stone, Soviet Agent–Case Closed," Haynes, Klehr, and Vassiliev write: "To put it plainly, from 1936 to 1939 I. F. Stone was a Soviet spy." Haynes and Klehr have written about Stone for years. See, for example: John Earl Haynes and Harvey Klehr, *Venona: Decoding Soviet Espionage in America* (New Haven, Conn: Yale University Press, 2002), pp. 247-9.

[22] Herb Romerstein and Eric Breindel, *The Venona Secrets* (Washington, DC: Regnery, 2000), pp. 432-9.

[23] Kalugin added that Stone "changed in the course of time like many of us"; in other words, he did not remain a communist–but for a time he was a Soviet agent. Oleg Kalugin, *Spymaster: My Thirty-Two Years in Intelligence and Espionage Against the West* (NY: Basic Books, 2009), p. 80.

[24] Among others, see: M. Stanton Evans and Herbert Romerstein, *Stalin's Secret Agents* (NY: Simon & Schuster/Threshold, 2012), pp. 138-9.

[25] Anthony Lewis, "Onward Christian Soldiers," *The New York Times*, March 10, 1983.

[26] Karl E. Meyer, "The Elusive Lenin," October 8, 1985, p. A30. For my extended examination of this, see: Kengor, *Dupes*, pp. 383-90.

[27] See Paul Kengor, *The Crusader: Ronald Reagan and the Fall of Communism* (NY: HarperCollins, 2007), p. 198.

[28] Evans and Romerstein, *Stalin's Secret Agents*, p. 142.

[29] Edgar Snow, *Red Star Over China* (NY: Random House, 1968).

[30] Ibid, p. 17.
[31] Ibid, p. 90.
[32] Ibid, pp. 90-4.
[33] Ibid, pp. 95-6.
[34] Ibid, pp. 59, 82-3, 104, 345-6, 359-60, 368-9, 386, and 445.
[35] The latest figures of 70-million plus by Mao are recorded in the seminal work by Jung Chang and Jon Halliday, *Mao: The Unknown Story* (New York: Knopf, 2005). On Mao, the *Black Book of Communism* records 65 million dead.
[36] Che Guevara, "One year of combat," *El Cubano Libre*, January 1958.
[37] The definitive work on Matthews and Cuba is by Anthony DePalma, *The Man Who Invented Fidel: Castro, Cuba, and Herbert L. Matthews of The New York Times* (NY: Public Affairs, 2007).
[38] Herbert L. Matthews, "Cuban Rebel Is Visited in Hideout," *The New York Times*, February 24, 1957, p. 1.
[39] Hollander, *Political Pilgrims*, p. 236.
[40] Hollander, *The Survival of the Adversary Culture* (New Brunswick, NJ: Transaction Publishers, 1988), p. 218.
[41] Transcript, "World News Tonight," ABC News, April 3, 1989.
[42] "Notable Quotables," Media Research Center, March 7, 1988.
[43] Ibid.
[44] Stephane Courteos, ed., et al., *The Black Book of Communism* (Cambridge, Mass.: Harvard University Press, 1999), p. 663.
[45] Humberto Fontova, "Cuba's Free and Fabulous Healthcare," Townhall.com, February 23, 2010. In truth, the idea that Cuba has "impressive" infant mortality rates under Castro is a myth. Fontova's article is one of many demonstrating that this is patently untrue.
[46] Richard Grenier, "Fidel's Theme Park Going Out of Business," *Washington Times*, February 23, 1992; and "Notable Quotables," Media Research Center, December 23, 1991.
[47] For more examples, see: Mona Charen, *Useful Idiots* (Washington, DC: Regnery, 2003), pp. 173-85.
[48] Cliff Kincaid, "The Terrible Truth About Walter Cronkite," Accuracy in Media, July 20, 1999.
[49] Cronkite's acceptance of the award and speech that followed was captured by America's Survival and is posted at: http://www.youtube.com/watch?v=95Jfa05PLSI&feature=gv.
[50] Walter Cronkite, *A Reporter's Life* (NY: Random House, 1997).
[51] "Excerpts From an Interview With Walter Cronkite of CBS News," *Public Papers of the Presidents of the United States: Ronald Reagan* (Washington, DC: GPO, 1989), March 3, 1981.
[52] The document was originally published in the appendices of my two books, *The Crusader* and *Dupes*.
[53] See: Kincaid, "The Terrible Truth About Walter Cronkite."
[54] "Teddy, the KGB and the top secret file," *The London Times*, February 2, 1992.

[55] See: Paul Kengor, "The KGB and Kennedy," *American Thinker*, August 31, 2009.

[56] See: Kengor, *Dupes*, pp. 69-78.

[57] Cliff Kincaid, *Saving the World for Socialism: How Soviet Dupe and Communist Fellow Traveler Curtis MacDougall Trained Today's "Progressive" Journalists* (Washington, DC: America's Survival Inc., 2012).

[58] Curtis MacDougall, *Interpretative Reporting* (NY: MacMillan, 1972).

[59] William David Sloan, *Makers of the Modern Mind* (NJ: Lawrence Erlbaum Associates, 1990).

[60] Curtis MacDougall and Robert D. Reid, *Interpretative Reporting* (NY: MacMillan, 1987, ninth edition), p. 18.

[61] The file is posted at www.usasurvival.org.

[62] "Summary Report: Curtis Daniel MacDougall," June 30, 1954, FBI file.

[63] See: Kengor, *The Communist*, pp. 105, 114-16, 120, 144, 222, and 272.

[64] The ad ran in the July 3, 1948 edition of the *Star*.

[65] See these articles on MacDougall in the *Chicago Star*: "MacDougall back in Senate race," May 15, 1948; "Dewey, Truman face test in South, says MacDougall," July 17, 1948; and "Sen. Taylor to speak at State Fair PP Day," August 14, 1948.

[66] "Progressive Party hails new paper," *Chicago Star*, September 4, 1948.

[67] Max Friedman's below referenced piece for the Winter Soldier website calls Feinglass a "probable KGB agent of influence." Also see Trevor Loudon, *Barack Obama and the Enemies Within* (Las Vegas, Nevada: Pacific Freedom Foundation, 2011), pp. 194, 200, and 424.

[68] See: Max Friedman, "John Kerry: Ambition and Opportunism," WinterSoldier.com, April 19, 2007.

[69] On Axelrod and the Canters, see: Kengor, *The Communist*, pp. 112-15.

[70] This report is more commonly known as "Appendix IX," or "Appendix Nine." "Investigation of Un-American Propaganda Activities in the United States," Special Committee on Un-American Activities, House of Representatives, 78th Congress, Second Session, on H. Res. 282, App. Part IX, Vol. 1 (Washington, DC: GPO, 1944), pp. 340-55.

[71] Ibid, pp. 340-1.

[72] American Committee for Protection of Foreign Born Collection, Tamiment Library, New York University, Boxes 1 and 2.

[73] Ibid.

[74] See: "Investigation of Un-American Propaganda Activities in the United States," pp. 298 and 301.

[75] Abt said that Congressman Vito Marcantonio "was a friend of the Party but never a member." See: John J. Abt, *Advocate and Activist, Memoirs of an American Communist Lawyer* (Urbana and Chicago: University of Illinois Press, 1993), p. 117. Also see: Romerstein and Breindel, *The Venona Secrets*, p. 214.

[76] "Hugh DeLacy, Ex-Legislator Active in the Progressive Party," *The New York Times*, August 21, 1986.

[77] "Curtis D. Macdougall," *The New York Times*, November 13, 1985.

[78] For sources on these details, see: Paul Kengor, *The Communist: Frank Marshall Davis, the Untold Story of Barack Obama's Mentor* (NY: Simon & Schuster, Threshold, 2012).

[79] Kengor, *The Communist*, pp. 124-41, 154-64, and 193-203.

[80] Ibid, 129-34.

[81] Ibid, pp. 139-41 and 177-80.

[82] Ibid, pp. 11-15.

[83] Barack Obama, *Dreams from My Father* (NY: Times Books, 1995).

[84] Brian Friel, Richard E. Cohen, and Kirk Victor, "Obama: Most Liberal Senator in 2007," *National Journal*, January 31, 2008.

[85] Sudhin Thanawala, "Writer offered a young Barack Obama advice on life," Associated Press, August 2, 2008. The other AP piece, by the same reporter, was titled, "In multiracial Hawaii, Obama faced discrimination," May 19, 2008.

[86] David Maraniss, "Though Obama Had to Leave to Find Himself, It Is Hawaii That Made His Rise Possible," *Washington Post*, August 22, 2008.

[87] Jon Meacham, "On His Own," *Newsweek*, August 23, 2008.

[88] See: David Remnick, *The Bridge: The Life and Rise of Barack Obama* (NT: Knopf, 2010), pp. 94-6.

[89] Dana Milbank, "Obama as You've Never Known Him!" *Washington Post*, May 23, 2008.

[90] See: Cliff Kincaid, "The Wit and Wisdom of Herbert Romerstein," Accuracy in Media, May 13, 2013.

[91] *The Black Book of Communism* uses the figure of 100 million, but that includes a very low estimate of only 20 million deaths in the Soviet Union. Other recent estimates, including Alexander Yakovlev's *A Century of Violence in Soviet Russia* (Yale University Press, 2002), claim that Stalin alone killed 60-70 million, a figure consistent with earlier estimates by the likes of Alexander Solzhenitsyn. Beyond the Soviet Union, it is estimated that Mao may have been responsible for upwards of 70 million deaths in communist China. And these figures related strictly to communist deaths in the Soviet Union and China. They do not touch upon those in Cambodia, North Korea, Cuba, Ethiopia, Afghanistan, Eastern Europe, and elsewhere.

[92] The website that lists the signatories for Progressives for Obama is http://www.progressivesforobama.net/.

[93] Jacob Weisberg, "Cold War Without End," *The New York Times Magazine*, November 28, 1999.

[94] Adam Hochschild, "Berkeley: What We Didn't Know," *The New York Review of Books*, May 23, 2013.

[95] James Burnham said this in his classic, *Suicide of the West*, first published in 1964.

Made in the USA
Monee, IL
25 October 2020